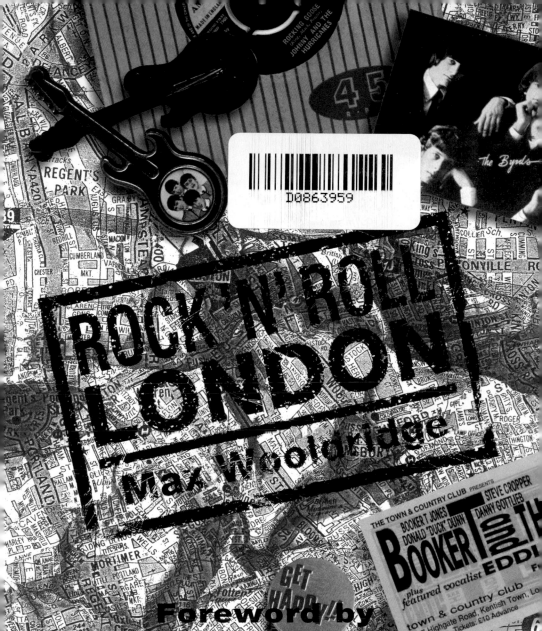

D0863959

ROCK 'N' ROLL LONDON

Max Wooldridge

Foreword by
MALCOLM MCLAREN

St. Martin's Griffin ※ New York

www.stmartins.com

ISBN 0-312-30442-0

First published in England by New Holland Publishers (UK) Ltd.
First U.S. Edition

10 9 8 7 6 5 4 3 2 1

Reproduction by Pica Digital Pte Ltd, Singapore
Printed and bound in Singapore by Kyodo Printing Co (Singapore) Pte Ltd

Cover and contents page photograph credits
Front cover: *the Rolling Stones* (Redferns) (tl), *the Boomtown Rats* (Ray Burmiston) (cr).
Spine: *Elvis Costello* (Keith Morris)
Opposite page: *Bob Marley* (Keith Morris) (tr), *the Middle Earth, Covent Garden* (Keith Morris) (cl),
the late Steve Clark of Def Leppard (Ray Burmiston) (br).

contents

Foreword

Rock'n'roll London's history cannot be told without its inextricable link to organized crime. The two go hand in hand. By 1945, London had become a state of anarchic chaos. The war had left it devastated and in ruins. Its people were starving and had little to celebrate. Victory was a hollow word. As the post-war era dawned, it brought a new breed of youth, and with a certain affluence by the dawn of the 50s, it brought the juvenile delinquent. The evolution of the teenager began in the war and their motto became 'Live Fast, Die Young'.

London's rock'n'roll map begins at this time. Catch the underground to South Ruislip, and here, in the remains of a mess hall on a now abandoned and converted US army base, GI's danced with English girls around a jukebox that screamed rock'n'roll's dirty lyrics. They reeked of free sex – sex that you could freely talk about. Songs such as 'Don't Tear My Clothes', 'The Honey Dipper', 'My Gal's a Jockey', and 'Lollipop Momma', were impossible to find in any record shop or hear on the radio. The jukebox boom, controlled by organized crime, acted like a quick-silver messenger service, and sent all of London's teenagers into a euphoric state that fulfilled the embodiment of their feelings and aspirations. It is therefore not difficult to understand how rock'n'roll London, due to its outlawed status, became a war cry for a new generation.

I was 15 when I found *Le Macabre* on Meard Street in Soho (a basement coffee house that used coffins as tables and skulls as lanterns), *Les Enfants Terribles* in Dean Street and *La Bastille* on Wardour Street. My favourite club, *La Discothèque*, on Wardour Street, owned by Rachman, the notorious slum landlord of Notting Hill, had brass beds and bare mattresses that lined the walls. It enabled most of us to experience sex, if we were lucky, for the first time. I wore Cuban heels to look as tall as possible so as an under-aged fan, I could squeeze into *La Saint Germain des Près* on Poland Street. The jukebox was the centre of attention at all these clubs and where I first heard 'Blue Moon' by the Marcels, 'Twist and Shout' by the Isley Brothers, and 'Please Mr. Postman' by the Marvelettes. Later, at the *Pigalle Club* in Piccadilly I saw the Beatles singing the same songs.

As an art student, I frequented the *Whisky A Go Go*, the *Flamingo* on Wardour Street, the *Scene* in Ham Yard, where I heard Screaming Jay Hawkins, Mary Wells, Georgie Fame, and the Animals. I would hang out on *Eel Pie Island* in Richmond all night, listening to a rhythm'n'blues band. Rock'n'roll had already become a far too commercial and exploited word. This was 1964. You stayed up all night drinking coke and taking purple hearts. The jukebox at the *Busy Bee Café* was a ritual for the Ton-Up biker gangs. They used it for a chicken run. Many lost their lives as they sped down the North Circular Road, trying to get back to the Café before the song on the jukebox ended. Sunday afternoons were spent watching the Rolling Stones at a jazz club in Great Newport Street in Soho. The *Railway Tavern* became a regular haunt on weekdays in Harrow. I discovered John Lee Hooker here. I was 18.

The teenager in the '60s had become a serious business, and one that was naturally exploited by an industry that was not always sympathetic. Carnaby Street, once dedicated to gay fashion, was now the sartorial playground for everyone, including tourists. It all began when someone decided to make a group of them: *Teenagers*, and in doing so, sell them bobby socks, lipsticks, garter belts, and deodorants – from fashion to music to movies. But what lay under it

Above: Vivienne Westwood and Malcolm McLaren in their King's Road shop.

was terrifying – our private culture and anti-world was fast being commercialized. Water would slowly be poured on the wine.

In 1976, punk rock blew up the established pop culture and all its pretensions. London was a battlefield again between the establishment and the new generations. 'Anarchy in the UK!' and 'God Save the Queen' were the anthems. I, the Sex Pistols and many others, became the new gangsters: Public Enemy Number One. Punk rock had failure programmed into its ideals. It was a noble pursuit, an idea that refused to lie down, refused to be commodified and sold. As nihilistic, as romantic and as creative as the outlawed teenage gangs of the '40s, we, the new anarchists, created a do-it-yourself culture, that invented groups that you could not fall in love with. For a moment, London was burning. The King's Road in Chelsea was punk's breeding ground and my shop, *Sex*, was its oasis. The club that was once called *Saint Germain Des Près* on Poland Street in Soho, was now called *Louise's*. It became the first punk club, a full-blown lesbian cruise joint and hangout for prostitutes, which was a recruitment centre for punk's chaotic army. The *El Paradise*, a strip club on Brewer Street, Soho, became the Sex Pistols' stage on Sundays. The *100 Club*, on Oxford Street became the site for a punk festival. London had never had it so good. Rock'n'roll London's '70s landmarks today remain buried under the dust of other façades.

The New Romantics and club culture of the '80s pushed the do-it-yourself aesthetic even further, making it faceless. The DJ became the new star, hidden in the shadows of the throbbing gristle of London's underground dance culture. A culture that had become more subversive and

Above: McLaren (left) and the Sex Pistols.

anticorporate than anything before, simply because there was nothing an industry could promote – nothing to market. But by the end of the 20th century it was finished. Everyone loves icons, and they were sadly missing by 2001.

The face of rock'n'roll London is difficult to find without a well-drawn and accurate volume such as this to record its history. The once Dickensian hovel and rehearsal room of those artful dodgers, the Sex Pistols, is nigh on impossible to find. It is hidden in the backyard at number 6 Denmark Street. Further along Denmark Street, towards St Giles, once stood *Regent Sound*, a dingy, small basement recording studio where the Rolling Stones made their first album. Denmark Street was London's Tin Pan Alley.

The counterculture of post-war America, which rock'n'roll London has merely mirrored, has collapsed. It may have spawned rock'n'roll music and inadvertently forced organized crime to make it successful. But having been digested and served back with equal force for the past 30 years, the culture has exhausted itself.

Rock'n'Roll London by Max Wooldridge lets you discover London's secret history of pop cultures, finds its tracings, haunts and landmarks. The book enables you to wander through the streets of London imagining and dreaming of that rock'n'roll chance rendezvous.

You will read about *Mezzo*, a restaurant on Wardour Street, where once stood the *Marquee*, rhythm'n'blues club, home to so many outlaws and heroes of another era. You might stop and wonder about those rock'n'roll ghosts that inhabit its basement. All that remains today is the occasional sighting of Bob Geldof nibbling *foie gras*. Back in the '70s, the Marquee opened its doors to the Sex Pistols for one chaotic night: Johnny Rotten was thrown off the stage. And the Sex Pistols were subsequently banned from ever playing at the Marquee again. Try dizzily crossing Abbey Road, where the Beatles once walked and imagine yourself rushing into the Abbey Road Studios to record.

All of these thoughts and memories provoked me to write a foreword for this fascinating, original and unique book that might just inspire those who study and read it to start the next cultural revolution.

Malcolm McLaren

Introduction

'Rain grey town, known for its sound'. The Byrds were not a London band but they were spot on about Britain's capital in their song 'Eight Miles High'. The perennial forecast may be cloudy periods between bursts of drizzle, but no one visits or lives in Britain's capital for the sunshine. London's roads are increasingly congested and Londoners are notoriously cold and distant unless you've been formally introduced. This place only really shines when the music starts.

While the British manufacturing industry may be on its deathbed, the country still leads the world in music. Los Angeles is sunnier and America invented rock'n'roll, but London has always been rock capital of the world. You can pretty much guarantee that every night in the back streets of some city or town far from England's capital, a lone singer with a badly tuned guitar is murdering a version of a song that started life in London. His command of English may not be good but you can bet he knows all the words to 'Streets of London' or 'Hey Jude'. For many foreigners, the first words of English learnt are the lyrics to Beatles' or Rolling Stones' songs.

If you've never seen four Japanese tourists trying to emulate the Fab Four on the famous zebra crossing near Abbey Road, I can assure you it's quite a sight and all the more surreal if they're walking backwards. However naff or uncool this may look to long-term London residents, it's only natural to want to tread softly in the footsteps of one's heroes. Finchley-born George Michael shared these precise sentiments when he paid £1.67 million for the piano on which John Lennon wrote 'Imagine'. But most mere mortals can't raise this kind of dosh and so have to pay homage the best way they can. And who blames them? Grown-up men may forget their wedding anniversaries but they'll never forget the first record they ever bought. In an increasingly uncertain world, music provides security and comfort. When our lives falter there's always the music we grew up with to fall back on.

In 1970, John Lennon sang 'There are places I remember, though some have changed'. He could have been talking about London today. Unfortunately, an assassin called Mark Chapman ensured he's not around to comment on how much London has changed. Coffee bars, chain pubs and bland office buildings now loom over the place of musical beacons. Many of the London rock landmarks fortunate enough to escape demolition are under new management. But at least some appear to be as invincible as ever, like Oxford Street's 100 Club,

Above: Boomtown Rat Bob Geldof: rising up in the music world.

which back in 1976 alternated between trad jazz gigs and hosting a punk rock festival. And if Freddie Mercury was still around would the Queen frontman even recognize his graffiti-covered former residence in Kensington?

It's unlikely that many Scousers will let us forget that the Beatles came from Liverpool – but everyone knows it was in London that they made their name. Likewise, Jimi Hendrix had to leave his native Seattle to flower in London. He expired here prematurely in a Marble Arch hotel suite. Elsewhere are the London rock shrines of Marc Bolan, Sandy Denny, Mama Cass and Keith Moon. Amazingly, the latter two died in the same Mayfair flat owned by Harry Nilsson,

their deaths just four years apart.

Central London is festooned with important rock'n'roll landmarks along roads such as Denmark Street, Wardour Street and Old Compton Street. But equally as important as Tin Pan Alley and Soho to London's rich musical history are its sprawling suburbs. While famous venues like the Marquee, the Speakeasy and the UFO club were musical magnets in the heart of town, London's musical lifeblood pulsed in its suburbs. The musical heritage of places like Bromley, Dartford, Ealing, Richmond and Muswell Hill may not be immediately apparent when you visit now, but they were traditionally the wellspring from which talent flowed into the centre. David Bowie came from Bromley, Elton John from Pinner and Rod Stewart and the Kinks from Muswell Hill. And without the suburbs there would have been no punk rock. Anonymous, semi-detached houses provided so much for youngsters to rebel against: the blandness, the boredom and the uniform conformity. Behind manicured front lawns frustrated teenagers have always wished they were somewhere else. That was usually uptown, some place miles away from Daddy-O, where things were happening and where they could dance with danger.

This book covers all the major spots in central and outer London that have made it the rock'n'roll capital of the world. Somehow a book called *Rock'n'Roll Home Counties* wouldn't quite have the same ring to it. For that reason we've ignored Woking, from where the Jam hailed. There are no descriptions of Eric Clapton's hideaway, Hurtwood Edge in Surrey, John Lennon's 72-acre Berkshire mansion, Tittenhurst Park, where he recorded 'Imagine', or Brian Jones's Crotchford Farm mansion, where he was found dead in his swimming pool. As for Pink Floyd's first singer and rock's most famous acid casualty, Syd Barrett, he now lives a reclusive life back in Cambridge – and that's just too far out, man.

Enjoy walking in the footsteps of your musical heroes. All we ask is that you respect the privacy of the current owners of houses where rock stars once resided. But as for Mezzo in Wardour Street, which replaced the world-famous Marquee club, go give 'em hell.

As Dartford's finest, Messrs Jagger and Richards once sang: 'You can't always get what you want... but you just might find you get what you need'.

Rock'n'Roll London

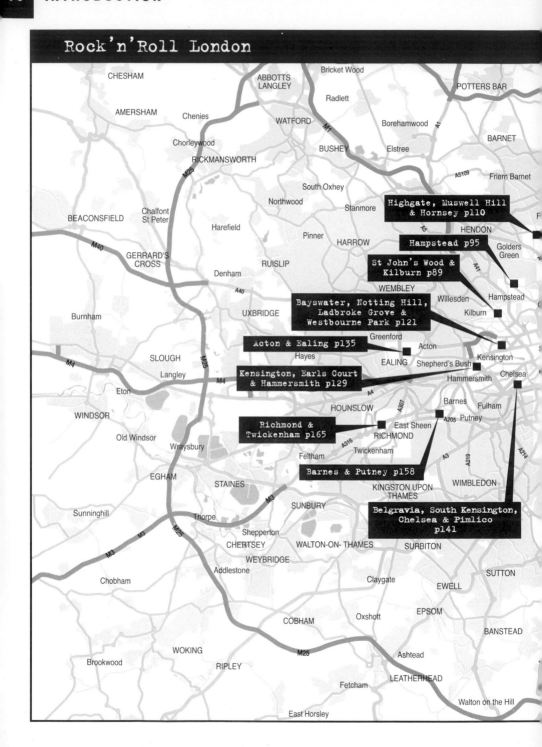

Highgate, Muswell Hill
& Hornsey p110

Hampstead p95

St John's Wood &
Kilburn p89

Bayswater, Notting Hill,
Ladbroke Grove &
Westbourne Park p121

Acton & Ealing p135

Kensington, Earls Court
& Hammersmith p129

Richmond &
Twickenham p165

Barnes & Putney p158

Belgravia, South Kensington,
Chelsea & Pimlico
p141

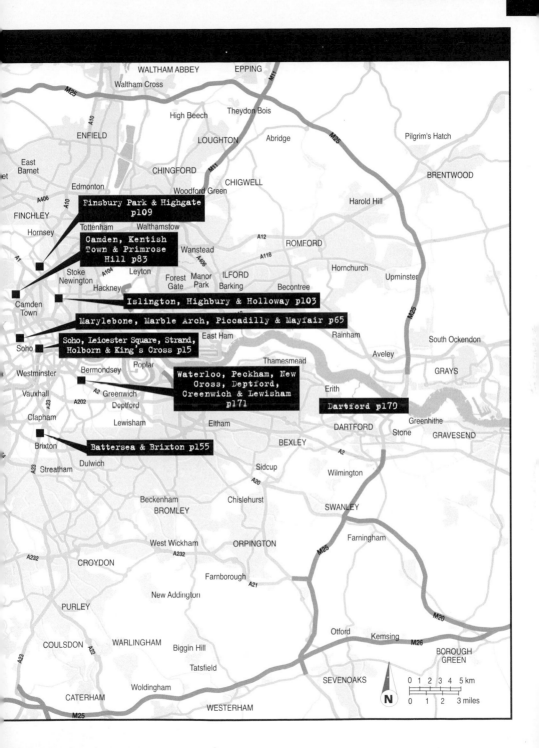

WALTHAM ABBEY EPPING
Waltham Cross

M25

A10

High Beech Theydon Bois

ENFIELD LOUGHTON Abridge Pilgrim's Hatch

M11

East
Barnet CHINGFORD CHIGWELL BRENTWOOD

Edmonton Woodford Green Harold Hill

A406 A10 **Finsbury Park & Highgate p109**

FINCHLEY Tottenham Walthamstow

Hornsey **Camden, Kentish Town & Primrose Hill p83** Wanstead A12 ROMFORD

A1 Stoke A104 Leyton Forest Manor ILFORD Hornchurch Upminster
Newington Gate Park Barking Becontree

Hackney **Islington, Highbury & Holloway p103**

Camden
Town **Marylebone, Marble Arch, Piccadilly & Mayfair p65**

A118 A406

Rainham South Ockendon

M25

Soho **Soho, Leicester Square, Strand, Holborn & King's Cross p15** East Ham Aveley

Westminster Bermondsey Poplar Thamesmead GRAYS

Waterloo, Peckham, New Cross, Deptford, Greenwich & Lewisham p171

Vauxhall A2 Greenwich Erith
A23 A202 Deptford **Dartford p179**

Clapham Lewisham Eltham DARTFORD Greenhithe
Stone GRAVESEND

Brixton **Battersea & Brixton p155** BEXLEY

Streatham Dulwich Sidcup Wilmington A2

A23 A20

Beckenham Chislehurst SWANLEY
BROMLEY

West Wickham ORPINGTON Farningham
A232 A232 M25

A232 CROYDON Farnborough
A21

PURLEY New Addington

A23 COULSDON A22 WARLINGHAM Otford Kemsing M26 M20

Biggin Hill BOROUGH GREEN

Tatsfield

Woldingham SEVENOAKS 0 1 2 3 4 5 km

CATERHAM N 0 1 2 3 miles
WESTERHAM

M25

CENTRAL

ive music and the thrill of the chase have attracted many wannabes to London's West End; the pursuit of a late night of wild abandon, unthinkable where they live. It's the chance to be part of the latest scene, or even better, the next best thing. Fickle, capricious, call it what you will, but the West End is the shop front where it happens. Enter the cosmopolitan mix of Soho and you've tapped into a defining spirit of tolerance; a den of artists, writers and worldly souls. There's an openness and acceptance of different ways and no pressure to conform.

Youth culture explosion!!! No sign of Daddy-o in this 1950s Soho coffee bar, rocking to the sounds of the Bellcats.

SOHO

Soho, a four-letter word that encompasses the essence of cool and everything exciting and vibrant. From the Blitz to the turn of the new millennium, anything happening in London has usually happened in Soho.

From jazz, skiffle and psychedelia to punk rock, Soho has been at the forefront of many musical explosions. After the war, basement jazz clubs arrived on the scene to meet the rising desire for entertainment in a battle-weary London. In the 1950s, teenagers flocked to the coffee bars, which had sprung up along Old Compton Street, to hear skiffle, Britain's very own rock'n'roll. The likes of Tommy Steele and the Shadows played sweaty, daytime venues to packed audiences. These were often so crowded that any member of the audience who fainted was simply pushed out through skylights onto the pavement. In the 1970s punk recreated this rebellious excitement, but with little of the charm.

Sadly, in recent years, Soho seems to have gone to sleep. It's still a creative hotbed, but there are precious few live music venues now. The rents have gone up, the area has been sanitized, but who knows what may happen should this ever-changing part of London awake from its slumber.

Key

1. Speakeasy
2. London Palladium
3. Marlborough Street Magistrates Court
4. Shakespeare's Head
5. Bag O' Nails
6. Prince of Wales Theatre
7. Scene
8. El Paradise
9. Jack of Clubs
10. Flamingo/W.A.G.
11. Ad Lib
12. Notre Dame 'The Venue'
13. Empire Ballroom
14. Hippodrome
15. Happening 44
16. Lee Ho Fook
17. 2 Is
18. Cecil Gee

19. Rocket Records
20. Round House
21. Marquee #2
22. Intrepid Fox
23. Bricklayers Arms
24. Trident Studios
25. Berwick Street/Noel Street
26. Vortex
27. 100 Club
28. Glitterbest
29. UFO
30. Horseshoe Hotel
31. Dominion Theatre
32. Dick James Music
33. La Giaconda
34. Helter Skelter
35. Saville Theatre
36. 6-8 Denmark Street
37. Astoria

38. St Martin's College of Art & Design
39. Pollo
40. Marquee #3
41. Cambridge
42. Le Kilt
43. Les Cousins
44. Ronnie Scott's
45. Bar Italia
46. Bunjies
47. Studio 51
48. Middle Earth
49. Rock Garden
50. Lyceum
51. London School of Economics
52. Roxy
53. Princess Louise
54. Rediffusion Studios
55. Water Rats
56. Shaw Theatre

Soho, Leicester Square, Strand, Holborn & King's Cross

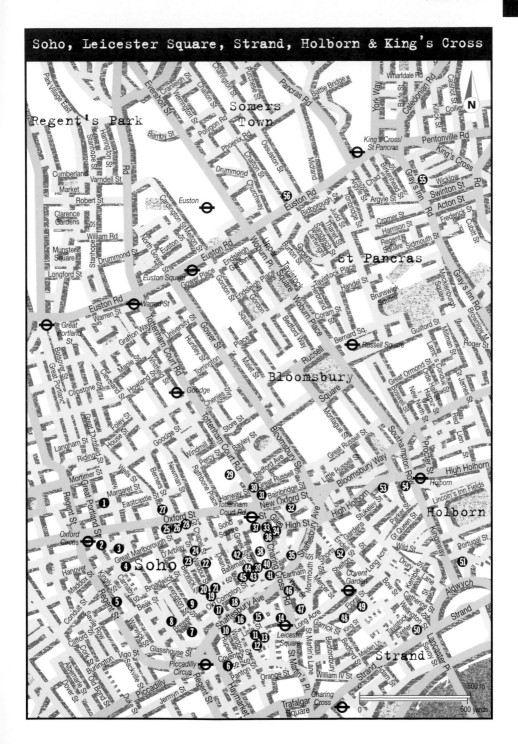

Left: Ronnie Scott's was and is more than just a jazz venue. Charlie Watts made an appearance in 2001.

Opposite: Jim Morrison at Ronnie Scott's. The serious drug and alcohol problems came later.

SOHO SQUARE

1 Soho Square still houses the headquarters of Paul McCartney's publishing empire, MPL Communications. Nearby, in the centre of Soho Square stands the statue of former British King, Charles II, and some local wit has noted that it bears a remarkable resemblance to the Rolling Stones' taciturn former bassist, Bill Wyman.

GREEK STREET

A popular folk hang-out during the 1960s was **Les Cousins**, an old skiffle cellar in the basement of 49 Greek Street, which had a fishing net draped over the stage. It was a cool place to be, if your idea of cool was being surrounded by men wearing black polo necks and corduroy jackets and with everyone sitting on the floor. Along with the Flamingo on Wardour Street, Cousins was one of the few places that stayed open all night in the early 1960s. There was one headline act every night, receiving as much as £5 in payment. Those who appeared regularly included Ralph McTell, John Martyn, Al Stewart, Roy Harper, Bert Jansch, Paul Simon and Yusuf Islam, the artist formerly known as Cat Stevens. Occasionally he picked up a guitar but was often too shy to play more than one or two songs.

FRITH STREET

Ronnie Scott's (see also Gerrard Street), the legendary jazz club, didn't transfer from Chinatown to its present location at 47 Frith Street until the week before Christmas in 1965. Sadly, the club proved to be the venue for Jimi Hendrix's last ever public performance on 16 September 1970, the night before he died of a drugs overdose. Hendrix came to see a gig by former lead singer of the Animals, Eric Burdon, and War. Hendrix jammed with Burdon on stage that night. The busy club owner renowned for his awful jokes – 'Pretend you're on the *Titanic*,' Scott used to tell audiences if he thought they needed livening up – also maintained a career as

Bright lights, big city: Soho in the 1960s.

Ford Zephyrs, the Bar Italia, sharp suits and Ronnie Scott's.

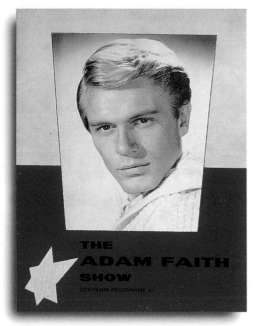

THE **ADAM FAITH** SHOW
SOUVENIR PROGRAMME 2

a saxophonist and bandleader. He provided one of the four saxophones on the Beatles' 'Lady Madonna', recorded at EMI's Abbey Road Studios in February 1968. Ronnie Scott committed suicide in December 1996, but his club, with its seductive, subdued crimson lighting, still attracts the big jazz names today.

Other London jazz venues may present star names, places such as the Royal Festival Hall and Camden's Jazz Café, but few can match the club's intimate setting right in the heart of Soho. Although Ronnie's enjoys a reputation as one of the leading clubs for jazz, its musical net has always been cast much wider. The Doors' Jim Morrison performed here and the Who premiered rock opera *Tommy* here to the press in 1970. Genesis were signed to Charisma Records label after boss Tony Stratton-Smith discovered them at Ronnie Scott's. In the early 1970s a second venue opened upstairs and extended a welcome to new and different performers. During the punk years, New Wave acts included Squeeze one night, followed by the Jam the next. Meanwhile, downstairs in the main club a more traditional fare featured the likes of Art Blakey, Horace Silver and Carmen McRae.

A bit of history lives on across the street in the form of **Bar Italia**, a sweet-smelling reminder of Soho's penchant for coffee bars of the mid-1950s and early 1960s. It is still one of London's great cafés and well worth a visit – especially when the Italian national football team are playing in a major international tournament. It knocks the spots off the ubiquitous coffee chain outlets that have flooded London in recent years.

Louie Brown, owner of the Scotch of St James, also ran **Le Kilt** club at 90 Frith Street. The venue featured a tartan carpet and was a popular nightspot of the 1960s. Beatles John Lennon and George Harrison came here in April 1966 to see the Lovin' Spoonful in concert. That night Harrison met Eric Clapton again, they'd met once before during the 1964–1965 'Another Beatles Christmas Show' at the Hammersmith Odeon.

OLD COMPTON STREET

Old Compton Street is the street that never sleeps, one of London's liveliest areas and one of the capital's foremost gay hang-outs. Back in the 1950s, it was all coffee bars and skiffle clubs that offered teenagers freedom, a cool atmosphere and no sign of Daddy-O. The coffee bar that billed itself as 'home of the stars' was the **2 Is** at 59 Old Compton Street. It's now a café chain outlet, but was a mecca for live jazz, skiffle and rock'n'roll bands in the 1950s. It became the best-known of the music coffee bars in the heart of Soho.

Opened in July 1956, the 2 Is was a launching pad for many musical careers and often the rocket was the impresario, Larry Parnes. It was a magnet for wannabe pop stars, a place where young hopefuls auditioned and many a teen idol was discovered. And what hopefuls they were. Cliff Richard, Adam Faith and Tommy Steele were all regulars here in the 1950s. Faith and Steele were discovered by Parnes, whose stable of rock'n'rollers included Marty Wilde and Billy Fury. The coffee bar's unusual name derived from the owners, three Iranian brothers who originally called it the 3 Is. When one of them left, they simply subtracted him from the name.

Soon after their arrival from Newcastle in September 1958, Hank Marvin and Bruce Welch were spotted at 2 Is and invited to join Cliff Richard's backing band, the Drifters (renamed the Shadows in July 1959). In the early 1960s, a young Marc Feld (later Marc Bolan) served drinks here and the coffee bar's jukebox helped nurture an early interest in American rhythm and blues. Peter Grant, larger-than-life manager of Led Zeppelin, also worked here as a bouncer.

Next door, at 57 Old Compton Street, was another coffee bar-cum-music venue then called Heaven and Hell. It was here that Hank Marvin, Bruce Welch and their band the Drifters played their first gig. This was also the place in which Harry Webb was reborn as Cliff Richard, a name-change courtesy of his manager John Foster.

Down the road is the cheap and cheerful **Pollo** pasta restaurant, at 20 Old Compton Street. Not only is this one of the best value restaurants in London, but it was a favourite haunt of former Pink Floyd frontman, Syd Barrett, who lived in nearby Earlham Street. In the late 1960s,

Opposite & below: Adam Faith and Marty Wilde were both regulars at the skiffle club the 2 Is.

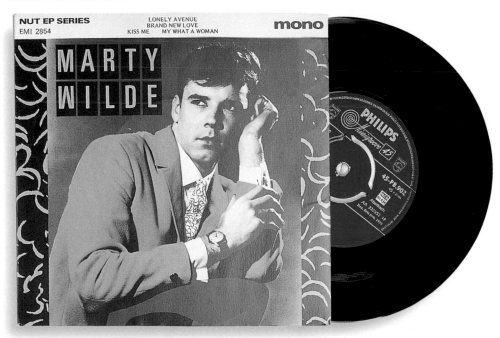

December 30, 1978   SOUNDS   Page 33

marquee

01-437 6603

90 Wardour St., W1

Thur 28th & Fri 29th Dec (Adm £1.60)
Marquee Christmas Spectacular
IAN GILLAN BAND
Plus guests & Joe Lung

Sun 31st Dec (Adm £3.00)
New Years Eve Extravaganza (7pm - 1am)
RADIO STARS
Autographs & Other Goodies
D.J. Jerry Floyd

Wednesday 3rd Jan (Adm £1.00)
EATER
Plus guests & Joe Lung

Sat 30th Dec (Adm £2.00)
NO DICE
Plus guests & Jerry Floyd

Monday 1st January 1979
CLOSED

Tuesday 2nd January (Adm £1.00)
TO BE ANNOUNCED
+ support & Joe Lung

Thursday 4th Jan (adm £1.00)
THE EDGE
Plus guests & Ian Fleming

HAMBURGERS AND OTHER HOT & COLD SNACKS AVAILABLE

Barrett was a regular diner here and Pollo looks like it hasn't changed much since his last visit.

Likewise, the Centrale Cafe on Moor Street, between Old Compton Street and Charing Cross Road, is where the Sex Pistols used to eat. With Formica tables and black benches, the Centrale looks just as it did in the 1970s, with prices to match. Nearby, the Victorian pub the **Cambridge**, named after its location on Cambridge Circus, was a favoured venue for the Sex Pistols. Its stained wood, polished brass fittings and full-length wall mirrors give the impression that it hasn't changed a lot since punk's heyday.

WARDOUR STREET

The original Oxford Street home of the **Marquee** (see also Oxford Street and Charing Cross Road) was a precursor to its second and most famous location at 90 Wardour Street, the venue of shows by the Who, the Rolling Stones and the Sex Pistols, among countless others. These large, ground-floor premises were previously a warehouse for raincoat maker Burberry. In its 24-year residency anyone who was (or wanted to be) anyone played here, including rhythm and blues pioneers Blues Incorporated, Jimi Hendrix, Pink Floyd, Queen, the Jam, the Police and every heavy metal band who ever fitted into spandex trousers. The Marquee's opening night on 13 March 1964, featuring Sonny Boy Williamson and the Yardbirds, set the scene for the shape of things to come. Over the years, both British and American groups played the Marquee club, among them Jethro Tull, Vanilla Fudge, Joe Cocker and punks such as the Damned. It was large enough to pack several hundred patrons in every night, but small enough to retain an atmosphere, unlike places such as Wembley Arena.

The Marquee was a regular gig for John Mayall's Bluesbreakers, Cream and Derek and the Dominos. Rod Stewart, who was spotted with Long John Baldry at the Marquee, soon signed a solo deal with Decca. Previously called the High Numbers, the Who left the mod clubs of Harrow and Acton and started a regular Tuesday residency at the Marquee in November 1964. After an enthusiastic review in *Melody Maker*, the queues along Wardour Street were soon snaking around the block. But the hippest Mod band of 1965 were called the Action and whenever they went to play in central London a parade of scooters would escort the group into town. They played the Marquee a total of 25 times and were sacked as the Who's support

Above: Backstage at the Marquee was where bands literally made their mark by adding their names to the walls of graffiti.

act by manager Kit Lambert for being too damn good. Former Genesis drummer, Phil Collins, was a huge fan and attended every Marquee gig they played. He cites them as a huge influence on Genesis. Many other bands played their first London gigs at the Marquee, including Led Zeppelin in October 1968, when they were still called the New Yardbirds. Their London debut featured an early rendition of 'Dazed and Confused', with guitarist Jimmy Page pioneering his unusual and eerie, violin-bow-on-guitar effect. The club advertised the gig as the Yardbirds, forgetting the prefix 'New'.

In the spring of 1966, musicians, poets and artists used to gather at the Marquee for Sunday afternoon sessions, called the Spontaneous Underground. These jams would prove highly influential and sowed the seeds for the psychedelic movement. Donovan turned up with sitars and congas and it was here that Pink Floyd first made their mark, abandoning jazz and blues in favour of their psychedelic sound. Often the group would grind to a halt in howls of echoes and feedback as they set the controls for an early psychedelic experience. Years later, the Sex Pistols filmed the promo clip for 'God Save the Queen' here, and Wardour Street became a hive of safety pins and bondage when they played their one and only gig at the Marquee as part of London's first punk festival in February 1976. It was their first major London gig as support to Eddie and the Hot Rods. Chairs flew as the Rods claimed the Sex Pistols had damaged their equipment. Rotten's crew were immediately banned from the venue by irate management and never invited back. The incident gained them valuable coverage in the music press, which no doubt

They took away paradise and put up a wine bar

COMMENTATATOR ON THE DEMISE OF THE MARQUEE

delighted their manager, Malcolm McLaren. He has since dismissed the building that replaced the Marquee as a symptom of 'the cappuccino culture'. The famous club was demolished to make way for Terence Conran's Mezzo restaurant, a move that sums up how much London has changed in recent years. The late-night smell of roadies lingering in the air along Wardour Street is now a distant memory. Only when the Marquee closed did people realize how important it was. Strange how you never really appreciate something until it's gone. 'They took away paradise and put up a wine bar,' an observer once commented plaintively in *Mojo* magazine.

When Covent Garden punk club the Roxy closed down, a much bigger club took over the mantle as the primary punk venue for central London. In July 1977, the **Vortex** opened on the

Below: Dave Vanian (centre) and the Damned were a regular attraction at the short-lived punk club, the Roxy.

premises of Crackers, 201 Wardour Street, near the corner of Oxford Street. The Jam paid homage to Wardour Street and the Vortex the following year in their 1978 track ' 'A' Bomb in Wardour Street', featuring the line, 'I'm stranded on the Vortex floor, my head's been kicked in and blood's starting to pour.' The site is currently a nightclub called Propaganda.

Any self-respecting punk would have gleefully gobbed on the doorstep of **Rocket Records**, a little down the road at 101 Wardour Street. In May 1973, Elton John set up his own record label after the successes of 'Crocodile Rock' and 'Daniel'. His instrumental hit 'Song For Guy' was written in 1979, an eulogy for Guy Burchett, a Rocket Records messenger who died in a motorcycle accident on the way to the office. Elton set up the Rocket label (now part of Island Records) to launch other artists, but the label's UK success came from his own releases.

Above: Formerly the Whisky A Go Go, the club became known simply as the Wag in the 1980s.

Opposite the entrance to Chinatown, the Whisky A Go Go, at 33-37 Wardour Street, opened in 1962. But in 1982 its name was abbreviated to the **W.A.G.** club, presumably to cater for stunned revellers unable to talk properly after being insulted by the wonderfully curt staff at Wong Kei (41 Wardour Street), a Chinese restaurant well known to Londoners. Downstairs was the **Flamingo** club, a live music venue and nightclub, which was a prime jazz nightspot in the 1960s. The club proved very popular with visiting black American GIs who much preferred the soul-based jazz of the music provided by popular resident house band, Georgie Fame and the Blue Flames. They made the break from rock'n'roll to jazz and emerged from the midnight-to-dawn All Nighters with the finger-poppin 'Yeh Yeh'. The Mingo, as it was often nicknamed, was owned by Rik and John Gunnell, who managed singing stars such as Chris Farlowe and Geno Washington. They also pioneered what was perhaps pop's first supergroup. Called Shotgun Express, it comprised Rod Stewart as singer, guitarist Peter Green and drummer Mick Fleetwood. The band split before the end of 1966, by which time the seeds were sown for the first line-up of the hugely successful Fleetwood Mac.

The studios of the Beatles' photographer, Dezo Hoffmann, were located on the second floor of 29 Wardour Street between 1960 and his death in March 1986. He photographed the Fab Four at his studios at four separate sessions between April and July 1963. In the 1960s the ground floor was the Romanella pizza restaurant. Not changing its spots much, the building is now owned by a pizza chain.

After flats in Ealing and Belgravia, the Who's guitarist and songwriter Pete Townshend lived in the top floor flat of 87 Wardour Street in the mid-1960s. During his tenure here he made part of the flat into a studio.

For anyone who believes that London has been taken over by endless Irish theme pubs and characterless chain bars, the **Intrepid Fox** at 99 Wardour Street comes as a breath of fresh air. As a dingy, alternative, punk and goth pub it's quite a contrast to nearby Mezzo. In the large downstairs bar the walls are covered with peeling

Above: The Intrepid Fox still retains its musical links and an individuality of character that is lacking in many pubs today.

posters of Jimi Hendrix, the Rolling Stones, the Who and the Sex Pistols. Punk classics, as well as Marilyn Manson and Sisters of Mercy, can still be heard blasting out of the speakers. It was in this boozer in the heart of Soho that Ronnie Wood first met Rod Stewart.

St Anne's Court, off Wardour Street, is one of those small, narrow, blink-and-you-might-miss-it alleyways that central London conjures up so well. It's a convenient cut-through to Dean Street and housed the former premises of **Trident Studios** (17 St Anne's Court) until 1984. While most of the Beatles' recordings were engineered at Abbey Road's famous studio number two, ironically, most of *Abbey Road* was recorded at these Soho studios. The Beatles utilized Trident extensively in 1968 because it was the first independent studio in England to have recording facilities that allowed eight separate sound sources to be recorded at the same time (eight-track); Abbey Road could only record four at a time. The Beatles also recorded 'Hey Jude' and other songs from *The White Album* here.

Ringo Starr and George Harrison came to Trident to produce songs for their solo albums. Ringo's *Sentimental Journey* and Harrison's *All Things Must Pass* came to life here, as did Lou Reed's *Transfomer* in 1972. His friend, David Bowie, came to the studio to record *Hunky Dory*, *Ziggy Stardust* and its much-anticipated follow-up *Aladdin Sane*. Elton John also recorded here before he hit superstardom and was forced to record overseas due to tax regulations. Producer Gus Dudgeon arrived with the musician to complete three albums, taping three songs per session because the studios were so expensive. Its resident piano turned out to be quite a star in itself. Not only was it used on 'Hey Jude' by the Beatles, but also by Elton John on 'Goodbye Yellow Brick Road' and on Queen's 'Bohemian Rhapsody'. In June 1969, David Bowie recorded 'Space Oddity' at Trident on the same day he signed a deal with Mercury Records. The venerable Trident received Genesis to record *Trespass*, their first Charisma album, in July 1970. Supertramp's first hit album, *Crime of the Century,* was recorded in 1974.

In the summer of 1954, one of London's first blues and skiffle clubs, the London Skiffle Centre, reopened as the Blues &

Above: Carnaby Street swung with fashionable wannabes but Wardour Street was where musicians hung out in pubs like the Ship.

Barrelhouse Club in a room above the former **Round House** pub, 83–85 Wardour Street, at the corner of Brewer Street. With an initial audience of about three – it could hold up to 125 people – the venue soon became more popular. On some nights, there were often more people waiting to play than pay. Muddy Waters was an early performer here.

BERWICK STREET

While the Beatles chose a zebra crossing in north London for one of their most memorable album covers, Oasis paid homage to the Fab Four a quarter of a century later at a street corner in Soho. The Gallagher brothers chose the intersection of **Berwick Street** and the aptly-named **Noel Street** to adorn the cover of their 1995 best-selling album *(What's the Story) Morning Glory?*.

While her teenage son ventured into more fashionable Soho haunts, Marc Bolan's mother, Phyllis Feld, manned a fruit and vegetable stall in Berwick Street market, which still thrives today. On the site of 44 Berwick Street was a coffee bar and skiffle club called the Freight Train – this later became a record shop called Musicland, where Elton John is said to have worked at weekends just to be around records.

POLAND STREET

The home of early punk was a lesbian bar called Louise's in Poland Street, Soho, where the real hardcore Sex Pistols crowd (the Bromley contingent with Siouxsie Sioux and Vivian from the Slits) went. The Pistols themselves came too. They were guaranteed a bit of peace and quiet here – if they went to the 100 Club or the Roxy they were likely to be mobbed.

ARGYLL STREET

In March 1964, Beatles manager Brian Epstein moved his fast-expanding North End Music Stores (NEMS) Enterprises to a suite of offices on the fifth floor of Sutherland House at 5–6 Argyll Street, next to the prestigious London Palladium. Originally at 13 Monmouth Street, Epstein moved to larger premises as the Beatles became more successful. The subtle boast of the company's headed notepaper stated: 'The finest and most efficient management/direction of artistes in the world'. The Sutherland House offices were also used by the Beatles for meetings and interviews with the press. In March 1966, John Lennon told an *Evening Standard* journalist the band were 'more popular than Jesus'. The comment caused outrage in the US, where the band were due to tour. Americans banned their records and those paragons of liberalism, the Ku Klux Klan, threatened to kill the band. NEMS remained in Argyll Street until a few months after Epstein's death in August 1967, when it moved to 3 Hill Street in Mayfair. Elvis Costello's mother, Lillian MacManus, once worked in Brian Epstein's NEMS shop in Liverpool and managed the record department in Selfridges, Oxford Street.

It was still known as the Palladium Theatre when the great Louis Armstrong played at 7 Argyll Street in 1932 and Duke Ellington and his Orchestra put it on the map the following year.

Built in 1910 by Frank Matcham on the site of a skating palace that dates back to 1870, it was officially renamed the **London Palladium** in 1934. The interior has been preserved and remains virtually identical today. For many the venue is synonymous with Sunday nights thanks to Val Parnell's 1960s television show, *Sunday Night at the London Palladium*, transmitted live from the theatre. The Beatles' appearance on this show in October 1963 brought them widespread fame in Britain. The audience went crazy and newspapers used the term Beatlemania the next day for the first – but not the last – time. The zenith of the young Rod Stewart's musical career came in August 1964 when he appeared at the Palladium on the same bill as the Rolling Stones for two shows. A year later the Stones returned, backed by the Walker Brothers. Because of his

Above: A star-studded line-up graces this London Palladium programme.

Above: The eternally youthful Cliff Richard has had a career spanning a number of decades, earning him world renown and a knighthood.

Right: Dedicated followers of fashion in Carnaby Street: yes, at least their mothers loved them.

drug reputation former Velvet Underground frontman Lou Reed failed to get to the London Palladium in 1977 and had to wait until 1989 to tread the boards. It remains one of London's top venues today. A month before he died of cancer in March 2000, a courageous Ian Dury played his final sell-out gig at the London Palladium while attached to a drip. Once memorably described as a cockney Kurt Weill, Dury fell out of fashion in the 1980s, with the decline of punk and the rise of the New Romantics. Never too concerned about his personal wealth and true to his principles, Dury once turned down an offer from Andrew Lloyd Webber to write the lyrics for *Cats* (a commission that reportedly earned millions for lyricist Richard Stilgoe). Dury had a simple explanation for rejecting Lloyd Webber's lucrative offer: 'I can't stand his music.'

CARNABY STREET

From 1964, this obscure seventeeth-century byway became a symbol of Swinging Sixties London, when dedicated followers of fashion headed here. Carnaby Street was the capital's fashion mecca and many designers and retailers opened up boutiques here to cash in on the surge in youth fashion. Like strolling peacocks, beautiful young things paraded along in the latest gear, be it roll-neck mini dresses, pop-art mini skirts or kinky boots. Young men cut a dash

Brel The Rolling Stones CS 167

Above: Mick Jagger looks a picture of restraint, Keith Richards turns gormlessness into an art-form and Charlie Watts looks like an extra from 'Star Trek'.

in penny loafers and suits so sharp you could cut yourself. It was on Carnaby Street that Mary Quant designed and sold the very first mini skirt, a simple dress that terminated four inches above the knees. Carnaby Street was the inspiration for the Kinks's classic 'Dedicated Follower of Fashion'. In the 1950s, the singer Vince Taylor (later David Bowie's inspiration for the Ziggy Stardust character) ran his own short-lived coffee bar called the Top Ten Club, at 50 Carnaby Street. The Clash would later cover his 'Brand New Cadillac' on their *London Calling* album. In the 1970s the offices of the *New Musical Express* were at 5–7 Carnaby Street. During the following decade, Neil Tennant of the Pet Shop Boys worked as editor of *Smash Hits* magazine, the offices of which were housed at 52–55 Carnaby Street. The street's most popular pub in the 1960s was probably the **Shakespeare's Head**, just off the main shopping area at 29 Great Marlborough Street, at the north end of Carnaby Street. In his candid autobiography, Kinks guitarist Dave Davies says the pub was a great place to score some drinamyl (purple hearts) or cannabis on Friday nights. When the pubs closed he would go on to Soho nightspots like the Whisky A Go Go (see Wardour Street) or the Flamingo (see Wardour Street).

Opposite Carnaby Street's junction with Great Marlborough Street was a building which was itself almost a regular venue on the rock'n'roll circuit. Every rock star worth their weight in fan mail made an appearance here at one time or another, including Brian Jones, Mick Jagger, Marianne Faithfull and Johnny Rotten. A compulsory West End haunt for any self-respecting bad-boy rocker, **Marlborough Street Magistrates Court**, 21 Great Marlborough Street, which closed in 1998, played host to scheduled appearances by rock stars, inevitably on drug possession charges. In the 1960s Mick Jagger and Brian Jones of the Rolling Stones both received fines for possessing cannabis. A few years later, fellow Stone Keith Richards was up on a similar charge, for heroin, firearms and ammunition possession. Johnny Rotten also paid a courtesy call in 1977 when he was fined £40 for drug possession.

Back when it was the **Bricklayers Arms** pub, 7 Broadwick Street was where the Rolling Stones met. Founder Brian Jones first auditioned Mick Jagger and Keith Richards to join his blues band, the Rollin' Stones, in March 1962. Pianist Ian Stewart turned up first and impressed Jones with his work. Jagger and Richards arrived later and were hired because their attitudes were perfect. The new group rehearsed in various Soho pubs including this one.

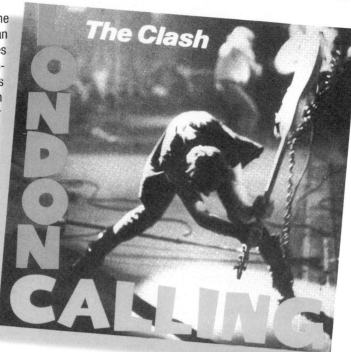

Above: The Clash wrote many songs about London and a couple of the best were on their album *London Calling* – to many, punk's last great album.

KINGLY STREET

Whenever Jimi Hendrix played the **Bag O'Nails** club, it quickly became a seething mass of people. Guitar heroes Pete Townshend, Jeff Beck, Jimmy Page and Eric Clapton all turned up to see Hendrix doing things with a guitar that had never been done before. Located in the basement of 9 Kingly Street, the Bag O'Nails club was a popular London nightspot when it opened in November 1966. The venue is probably most famous for being the place where Paul McCartney met a visiting New York photographer, Linda Eastman, on 15 May 1967, at a Georgie Fame and the Blue Flames gig. The two formed a steady relationship and were married in March 1969. Fleetwood Mac's John McVie proposed to Christine Perfect in the club too. A former jazz club that became a trendy rhythm and blues club, the Bag was one of the earliest examples of a danceband dive that grew up quickly around Soho in the 1930s. It ranks prominently in the history of British swing music and was the first rhythm club to be inaugurated in Britain. It became a meeting place where jazz enthusiasts could listen to live jam sessions and the

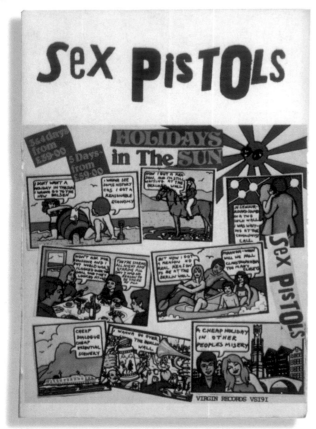

Above: When venues became hard to find the Sex Pistols had to play strip-joints such as El Paradise in Brewer Street.

latest American recordings. It also attracted those who wanted to come to a club to listen rather than dance. In the late 1960s, the Bag O'Nails was an international mecca for rock musicians, and hard as it is to imagine nowadays, on any given night one of the Beatles, the Rolling Stones or even Jimi Hendrix might turn up to relax and mix with other performers. Throughout much of 1967 and 1968, the Beatles were late-night regulars, especially after recording sessions at EMI's Abbey Road. Paul McCartney even had his own private table in the club. When a young Elton John played here with his Bluesology, headliner Long John Baldry was so impressed he hired them as a backing band on the spot. Elton later wrote 'Someone Saved My Life Tonight' about Baldry.

BREWER STREET

One David Jones – later to find fame after swapping the surname Jones for that of Bowie, because of the existing Davy Jones of the Monkees – performed his first professional gig in late 1964 at the **Jack of Clubs** (10 Brewer Street). He appeared with the King Bees, a rhythm and blues combo. The band stopped after just two songs due to the lack of interest from the audience.

By April 1976, the Sex Pistols' live performances were so notorious that it became harder for them to play any gigs. Malcolm McLaren secured them a gig in the heart of Soho's red-light district, at the premises of a sleazy strip-club called **El Paradise** at 24 Brewer Street. According to McLaren, the stage was the size of that of a Punch and Judy show and the whole place 'smelled like a shithole. But it looked good because it had this terrific entrance with these huge nude women in gilt frames.' Bassist Glen Matlock said McLaren had arranged the gig through the owners, some sort of Maltese gangster types. 'We had to take the seats out and get buckets of disinfectant and swab the place out. It was kind of crusty from all these punters shooting their wads.' Strippers were working before the Pistols went on stage and after they finished they started stripping again. 'We had about ten people watching us during the gig,' recalls Matlock. 'I stumbled and fell on the lights that were normally anchored above but were on the ground and burned myself really bad.' El Paradise proved too unstable a regular venue – even for the Sex Pistols.

GREAT WINDMILL STREET

Scooters were the preferred mode of transport to the **Scene**, the leading Mod nightclub in the centre of town at Ham Yard, 41 Great Windmill Street, near Piccadilly Circus. As a live venue, it catered first for jazz fans as Club 11, one of London's first modern jazz clubs. Clarinettist Cy Laurie's trad jazz club lasted until the early 1960s, when the basement hosted the Piccadilly Jazz Club, before the Mod movement claimed the rhythm and blues club as its own. Mod culture revolved around the Scene club: nice threads, sharp suits and more than the odd parka coat. It was unlicenced, but this hardly mattered to the pill-popping crowd. Ten shillings (50p) bought one hundred purple hearts (drinamyl), the fashionable amphetamine of the day. In December 1963, the Animals played their first London gig at the Scene, followed a few months later by a band called the High Numbers. Before the end of the year, they had changed their name to the Who. The Scene is now long gone.

> **We had about ten people watching us during the gig. I stumbled and fell on the lights that were normally anchored above but were on the ground and burned myself really bad.**
>
> GLEN MATLOCK, ON THE EL PARADISE STRIP CLUB GIG

SHAFTESBURY AVENUE

Opened in 1931, the **Saville Theatre**, at 135–139 Shaftesbury Avenue, was a part of London's theatreland until Beatles manager, Brian Epstein, took over the licence in 1965. At the end of 1966, he started staging Sunday evening rock concerts. They became a popular draw and it isn't hard to see why, with artists like Jimi Hendrix, Fairport Convention, Cream, the Who and Pink Floyd treading the boards. The venue managed to accomplish a rare feat: with a capacity of 1,200, it was large enough to be deemed important but was able to retain a club-like intimacy. After Epstein's death the following summer, the plug was pulled on the site as a rock venue and it reverted to a theatre. The venue was renamed the Shaftesbury Theatre, and it was here, in 1968, that the musical *Hair* opened, with Scots rocker Alex Harvey in the house band. In the 1970s the theatre was converted into a cinema and is owned by the ABC chain.

Music is so often inextricably linked with fashion and fans are defined by the clothes they wear. The fashion mecca for the elite of the 1960s (including a young Eric Clapton) was the **Cecil Gee** menswear shop at 39 Shaftesbury Avenue. Although no longer there, the shop was one of the first retailers to import clothing from Europe, adding a little sparkle into the previously dull world of British menswear. The store supplied threads to most of the bands of the day and caught the attention of Who drummer Keith Moon, who bought a gold lamé suit that he first saw in a window display. The shop's interior was suitably cool, with pictures of jazz musicians on the wall and a Gaggia coffee machine. In the 1960s, the shop advertised itself in the weekly music papers as: 'the only man's store in Europe catering for the professional artist and musician'. In 1989 the shop moved across the road. Needless to say, there's now no coffee machine nor a Cecil Gee shop for that matter.

GERRARD STREET

Any jazz-head who knows their stuff (and inevitably most of them do) will tell you that the first location of London's most famous jazz club, Ronnie Scott's (see also Frith Street), was at 39 Gerrard Street. In the mid-1960s it moved to its present-day premises in Frith Street, but the original was a good example of the jazz clubs that boomed in Soho after the war, a smoky basement with some guy playing a saxophone. It was a place where young people were determined to enjoy themselves and could go without being troubled. The club opened in October 1959 with headliners the Tubby Hayes Quartet. All four of the Beatles visited the Gerrard Street venue in the early hours of 9 October 1963. Here they celebrated John Lennon's 23rd birthday grooving to a performance by blind saxophonist Rahsaan Roland Kirk. The premises are now a Chinese supermarket in the heart of buzzing Chinatown.

Below: American singer, Warren Zevon, mentioned Lee Ho Fook in his classic song 'Werewolves of London'.

Another jazz dive was the **Happening 44** club (44 Gerrard Street), a basement club that also featured different styles of music. In the early 1950s you might have stumbled upon a gig by the West End Jazz Club, featuring George Melly, who sang with the resident Mick Mulligan Band. In the late 1960s, the club became a psychedelic venue to rival Covent Garden's Middle Earth club. North London folk-rock band Fairport Convention played audition nights at the club in 1967 and were soon spotted. They were originally influenced by West Coast rock bands like Jefferson Airplane, switching to their better known style when folk singer Sandy Denny and fiddler Dave Swarbrick joined the group. As you pass 15 Gerrard Street you may wish to call in and sample the fare of **Lee Ho Fook**, the Chinese restaurant that ended up in the lyrics to Warren Zevon's classic 'Werewolves of London'.

COVENTRY STREET

One of the Beatles' best-remembered concerts was at the **Prince of Wales Theatre** at 31 Coventry Street. For the 1963 Royal Command Variety Performance, the Fab Four performed in front of the Queen Mother and Princess Margaret. John Lennon's Scouse wit brought the house down with a stage request: 'For this next number we'd like to ask your help. Will the people in the cheaper seats clap your hands. The rest of you, if you'll just rattle your jewellery.' The Fabs appeared again at the Prince of Wales Theatre in May the following year, at a 'Pops Alive' concert, a series of Sunday gigs promoted by Brian Epstein.

> For this next number we'd like to ask your help. Will the people in the cheaper seats clap your hands. The rest of you, if you'll just rattle your jewellery.
>
> JOHN LENNON, 1963 ROYAL COMMAND VARIETY PERFORMANCE

CHARING CROSS ROAD

In 1988, the legendary **Marquee** club (see under Wardour Street and Oxford Street) moved from its Wardour Street address to its third and final incarnation at 105 Charing Cross Road with US heavy metal band Kiss headlining its opening night. Oasis, who played one of their last club shows here, was just one of many big names to keep the reputation of the Marquee going strong. It finally closed for good in 1996 and is now another outlet of the ubiquitous Wetherspoon pub chain, packed nightly with singletons and office workers. Now, the only sounds here are the incessant ringing of mobile telephones.

The not-so-cuddly fab four your grandparents warned you about, the Sex Pistols, played their first gig on 6 November 1975 at **St Martin's College of Art and Design**, 109 Charing Cross Road, a stone's throw from their Tin Pan Alley squat in Denmark Street. In fact, it was so close, they were able to carry their gear over the road. The college was a rendezvous for early punk groups and an apt choice as a first venue. The Pistols' bass player, Glen Matlock, was a former student, as was Malcolm McLaren, who studied life-drawing in 1963. He later transferred to graphics when his mother objected to the nudes on display. At that Sex Pistols' gig Johnny Rotten sported a Pink Floyd T-shirt with 'I hate' scrawled on it and they were supported by Bazooka Joe, an early outfit for Stuart Goddard (alias Adam Ant). The gig was not a great success in itself – the plug was pulled after five songs – but it didn't matter because

Above: The Marquee's last incarnation on Charing Cross Road; now it's mobile phones instead of rockers.

the Sex Pistols had made their mark. Rotten's old school friend John Beverley (later Sid Vicious) started a trend in the audience when he began jumping up and down, a dance that came to be known as pogoing. Another former St Martin's student is Jarvis Cocker of Pulp, who studied film-making here after turning down a place at Oxford University. Cocker name-checks his former college in 'Common People', one of Pulp's finest moments. PJ Harvey and Sade also studied here.

Not to be confused with the Finsbury Park Astoria (later to become the Rainbow), the **Astoria** at 165 Charing Cross Road remains a major West End venue. It has hosted gigs by Prince, Oasis, U2 and David Bowie. The Astoria was originally built as a Crosse and Blackwell pickle factory, before it was converted into a music hall offering rock concerts and club nights. In February 2001, Irish supergroup U2 played the Astoria in front of a sell-out 1,800 crowd. Tickets for the gig changed hands for as much as £2,000 on the black market.

Above: Adam and the Ants at the Astoria. Adam Ant's first band, Bazooka Joe, supported the Sex Pistols' first gig at St Martin's College.

Right: The Astoria on Charing Cross Road, not bad for an old pickle factory!

During one of his first UK visits, in January 1963, Bob Dylan played in the basement of the former Dobell's Music Shop at 77 Charing Cross Road. He recorded under the name Blind Boy Grunt on an album by folk singer Richard Farina. Dobell's was a popular jazz and blues record shop and much-loved by a young Eric Clapton.

On the other side of the street, at 132 Charing Cross Road, an important meeting took place in November 1962.

The Beatles manager, Brian Epstein, came here to discuss a music publishing deal at the offices of Dick James Music. Epstein was impressed and soon signed along the dotted line.

Guitar heroes often hot-footed it to 114-116 Charing Cross Road, Selmer's music shop. When it was still called Lew Davies, Eric Clapton bought his first Gibson guitar here. Dave Davies of the Kinks also bought his first guitar on hire purchase from the shop and worked as an apprentice in the workshop, repairing brass and woodwind instruments. In his lunch breaks he held jam sessions in the lathe room. Brian Jones's replacement in the Rolling Stones, Mick Taylor, got his first Les Paul guitar at Selmer's sold to him by a young sales assistant called Paul Kossoff. Later the guitarist with Free, Kossoff was to die of a drugs overdose aboard an aeroplane over the Atlantic in 1976.

DENMARK STREET

Traditionally, Denmark Street, London's Tin Pan Alley, was the heart of the music business from the 1940s to the 1960s. Music shops, publishers and labels formed the headquarters of the industry that crowded on Denmark Street. Nowadays, Tin Pan Alley is still music-orientated but

Opposite: Not to be confused with that bloke from Peters and Lee; Mr Robert Zimmerman, alias Bob Dylan.

Below: A music shop on Denmark Street otherwise known as Tin Pan Alley. A number of shops catering for all music aficionados can still be found.

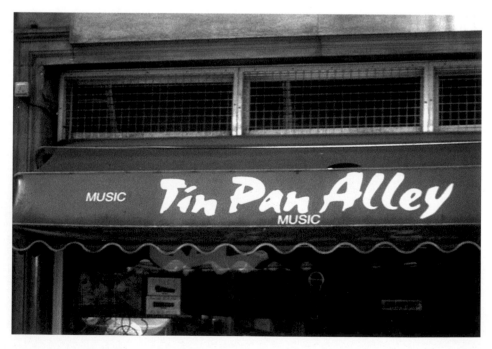

it is the home of guitar and keyboard shops rather than decision-making executives.

Long before he wore knee-length boots and silly glasses, Elton John worked in the offices of Mills Music, a music publisher located at 20 Denmark Street. It was his first job after leaving Pinner County Grammar School in 1963. He became an office boy and general help at a weekly salary of four pounds. Not much, but at least it gave him a foot in the door. He worked here for 18 months while playing at night in his band, Bluesology.

One of the most popular music industry haunts in the Swinging Sixties was **La Giaconda** (9a Denmark Street). Here, in October 1965, the Small Faces decided on their name and turned professional by signing a record deal with Decca. Regulars Marc Bolan and David Bowie made the big time too, but there were plenty of others who didn't. For years it was a café called Borona but has reverted to La Giaconda once again.

In the early days of punk, at the end of 1975, three of the Sex Pistols moved into an attic flat, above **6-8 Denmark Street**, rented for them by manager Malcolm McLaren. 'It was an absolute hovel,' McLaren said years later. Despite the lack of sanitation the Pistols were quite happy with it. And, according to Jon Savage in his excellent book, *England's Dreaming*, 'Johnny Rotten liked the flat because it was dank and depressing; Steve Jones liked it because he now had a W1 address.' McLaren also rented a ground floor rehearsal room at the back of the building, where the band fine-tuned their sound and ran through favourite songs by the Who and the Small Faces. Steve Jones, Paul Cook and Glen Matlock lived in the flat and Johnny Rotten joined them when he wasn't squatting in Hampstead High Street. Their first hits, 'Anarchy In The UK' and 'Pretty Vacant', were two of seven songs recorded in July 1976 in the rehearsal room. A year later, Siouxsie and the Banshees wrote their first song, 'Love in a Void', here.

A classic rock landmark is 4 Denmark Street, the former premises of Regent Sound Studios, a popular and relatively inexpensive place for musicians to make tapes of their work. In January 1964, the Rolling Stones held their first recording session here, covering Buddy Holly's 'Not Fade Away'. It was their first UK top three hit. The studios were also the site for the Kinks' debut session that same month. They recorded 'It's Alright', 'One Fine Day' and 'I Believed You', which landed the band a recording contract with Pye Records. Both records were produced by Shel Talmy, the Who's American producer. In late 1967, Genesis recorded their first single 'Silent Sun' at Regent Studios, financed by the musical impresario, Jonathan King, a former student of Charterhouse school in Surrey, where the band formed and were still students. Genesis had been called the Anon until teenagers Peter Gabriel and Mike Rutherford sent a demo tape to King, who renamed the band and wangled a one-year deal with Decca. Long departed from Denmark Street is the weekly paper *New Musical Express*, which started life at no. 5 but now forms part of the huge IPC publishing empire in Stamford Street, near Waterloo. But, there is still plenty of rock'n'roll writing to be found at no. 4. Today the premises are occupied by **Helter Skelter**, the best bookshop specializing in rock and pop music in the UK, if not the world.

LITCHFIELD STREET

During another early visit to the UK, in 1962, Bob Dylan dropped into **Bunjies** at 27 Litchfield Street, a well-known folk club and coffee bar. He paid an entrance fee like any punter and sang a couple of songs. The venue first opened in the mid-1950s, making it an earlier arrival on the

Above: La Giaconda. In the 1960s all the wannabes flocked here hoping to make it on the music circuit.

scene than that other great folk bastion, the Troubadour, in Earl's Court.

Bunjies attracted liberal-minded beatniks desperate to escape their parents, exchange views and guitar-accompanied songs. Into this free-spirited world of the early 1960s entered former football apprentice Rod Stewart, Scottish folk singer Al Stewart (no relation) and New Yorker Paul Simon, who had quit a law course in New York to come to Europe. A few years later, a cash-strapped Simon would offer to sell Al Stewart his entire catalogue of songs for £5,000. It contained classics like 'Homeward Bound', 'I Am A Rock' and 'The Sound Of Silence', but Stewart couldn't raise sufficient money.

COVENT GARDEN

In the wake of the original hippy sanctum, the UFO club (see Tottenham Court Road and Chalk Farm), another psychedelic haven blossomed in the heart of Covent Garden in 1967. Originally a seventeeth-century music hall, the **Middle Earth** club, at 43 King Street, formerly the Electric Garden, was renamed as a homage to the location of JRR Tolkien's *Lord of the Rings*. Middle Earth was a hippy's wet-dream, an underground basement club filled with wafts of incense, strobe-lighting, oil wheel light shows, wall-to-wall hippies, plenty of mind-altering drugs and, oh yes, a bit of music. Located near the Opera House, the venue played host to Pink Floyd and the

Nice (featuring Keith Emerson on keyboards) and saw the UK debut of Captain Beefheart and his Magic Band. It hosted all-nighters on Fridays and Saturdays when the main band came on at about 3 a.m. Marc Bolan made the underground venue his second home during the winter of 1967-68, when he hung out with his friend and resident DJ John Peel. The venue was still used as a fruit and vegetable warehouse, with pineapples and bananas stocked in the corner. The market porters took a dim view of the happenings and the strange smells emanating from the gates of Middle Earth, not to mention the stoned freaks dressed in long kaftans and sporting weird expressions. Middle Earth suffered constant harassment from the authorities. At a private party one night in March 1968, one guest brought along their kids, 150 police raided, found the children and told the Covent Garden porters that the hippies were crucifying children. The porters wasted no time in promptly smashing the place up and Middle Earth was forced to move out of Covent Garden to the Roundhouse (see Chalk Farm). In August 1965, a young Eric Clapton lived in the flat of poet Ted Milton, at 74 Long Acre. The flat was situated above a fruit wholesaler called Mash and Austin.

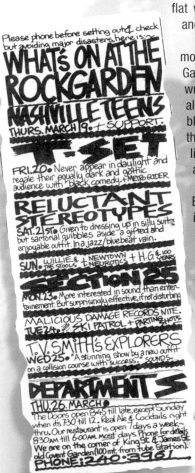

In early 1966, Pink Floyd frontman Syd Barrett moved from Highgate to 2 Earlham Street in Covent Garden. His songwriting powers were at a peak and he wrote much of the material for the first two Floyd albums. It was here he named the band after two bluesmen, Pink Anderson and Floyd Council. Barrett left the band in 1969 after a bout of mental illness. He now lives as a recluse in Cambridge, shuns his cult status and never plays the guitar.

Just along from the old building that housed Middle Earth is the **Rock Garden**, at 6-7 The Piazza. It opened in 1976 on the corner of James Street and King Street, and remains there today. It's still a popular live music venue and it was here that the Smiths made their London debut in March 1983. On the strength of their show, they were signed to the Rough Trade record label.

Pogoing, going, going, gone. Like everything about punk, the **Roxy** was short-lived. For three months between January and April 1977, the hardcore of London's punks found some salvation at this venue located at 41–43 Neal Street. At last they could hang out at London's first club totally dedicated to punk and once again see the bands

Opposite: A psychedelic heaven: the Nice at the Covent Garden hippy venue, Middle Earth.

live, after their heroes had been banned from playing virtually everywhere else. The small basement club was run by Vivienne Westwood's former accountant, Andy Czezowski, and opened on New Year's Day 1977 with a gig headlined by the Clash. Lead singer Joe Strummer wore a customized white shirt emblazoned with a massive '1977' on the front. Also on the bill was Chrissie Hynde of the Pretenders making her live UK debut with the Johnny Moped Band. The Jam played an early date at the Roxy and the Damned became a regular attraction. Before the pirate gear Adam and the Ants made their debut at the club's closing night party on 23 April 1977. Playing on the same bill were Siouxsie and the Banshees and it was here that their guitarist Marco Pirroni met and became firm friends with Stuart Goddard. They later reformed the group after the Ants deserted Stuart for Malcolm McLaren's Bow Wow Wow.

GREAT NEWPORT STREET

An influential jazz club of the Sixties called **Studio 51** was located at 10–11 Great Newport Street. Now long closed, it was an early gig for the Rolling Stones, who hosted regular Sunday afternoon and Monday evening shows here in late 1963 while seeking to build on the success of their first hit, 'Come On'. Brian Jones kept teenagers transfixed with his harmonica routines and the band's earthy brand of rock'n'roll was then closer to rhythm and blues. This Great Newport Street basement dive enjoyed various identities after it opened as a music venue in May 1951. Trumpeter Ken Colyer launched a successful revivalist jazz club here in 1954, playing purist traditional jazz before rhythm and blues infiltrated the jazz clubs in a big way. Rod Stewart played harmonica here with a band called Jimmy Powell and the Five Dimensions and the Yardbirds, with new guitarist Eric Clapton on board, improvised at the club when they took over the Rolling Stones' residency.

Above: Jazz greats never die but are remembered in stone. Ken Colyer's plaque in Great Newport Street.

Left: The Belle Stars at the Rock Garden, a venue still going strong in the heart of Covent Garden.

LEICESTER SQUARE

Paul and Linda McCartney threw a party at the **Empire Ballroom**, located at 5-6 Leicester Square, in November 1971 to celebrate the launch of the band Wings. Just around the corner from Leicester Square, former Beatles' drummer, Ringo Starr, proposed to his first wife, Maureen Cox, at the **Ad Lib**, 7 Leicester Place, a popular in-crowd nightspot of the 1960s. The club was at the top of the building, which also housed the offices of the council refuse collection. A small lift was the only way to reach the club. Visitors, including the pop elite, fashion designers such as Mary Quant and Jean Muir and young actresses Hayley Mills and Julie Christie, were greeted by mirrors, fur-lined walls and tanks of piranha fish. For a while, the Ad Lib was the in-place. In those days the credibility of a place was largely determined by whether the Beatles went there or not and perhaps the Ad Lib is best known as the nightclub where John Lennon and George Harrison went in 1965 apparently after taking LSD for the first time. Their drinks were allegedly spiked earlier in the evening whilst at the flat of a dentist friend.

At 5 Leicester Place is the Roman Catholic Church, the Notre Dame de France, an unlikely venue for some riotous Sex Pistols gigs in the mid-1970s. The dance hall beneath the church temporarily solved the Pistols' perennial problem of being banned from most venues. As the Notre Dame Hall wasn't part of the rock scene, manager Malcom McLaren had no trouble getting the green light to play there. Today the place looks the same as it was when the Pistols competed for top billing with ballroom dancers. A London Weekend Show TV documentary about punk was filmed in the building, now called **Notre Dame 'The Venue'**.

Just off the Charing Cross Road entrance to Leicester Square, at 10 Cranbourn Street, is a venue now called the **Hippodrome**, a name only revived in the early 1980s. Long before it became one of London's best-known nightclubs with beefy bouncers attuned to turning away beered-up lads from the suburbs, it was a popular cabaret venue called the Talk of the Town. Punters could dine and watch top international singers and musicians perform live. The building itself dates back to the turn of the twentieth century and was a venue as early as 1919. Designed by Frank Matcham (who also created the London Palladium) the Hippodrome's distinctive architectural feature is the statue of a horse-drawn chariot on its roof.

STRAND

Between 1945 and the mid-1980s, the **Lyceum** on Wellington Street, just off the Strand, was one of London's foremost live music and dance hall venues. Located close to Waterloo Bridge, the Lyceum covered a range of music, from its grand origins right through to a warm embrace of punk. It was originally built as an opera house in 1834, but by the late 1970s Sex Pistols' lead singer, Johnny Rotten, was stubbing cigarettes out on his forearm on stage. During the second wave of punk rock, which launched bands like X-Ray Spex and the Adverts, Sunday nights were

Right: Bob Marley and the Wailers breakthrough album *Live!* was recorded at the Lyceum in 1975.

dedicated to punk evenings at the Lyceum. The only spiky hair on display today is on the costumes of characters in the Disney show *The Lion King*. John Lennon played his last live gig in England here in December 1969, appearing on stage with the Plastic Ono Band as part of a UNICEF Peace For Christmas benefit concert. Earlier that summer, Keith Emerson's band, the Nice, topped the bill at a Midnight Court gig with support from Yes, Renaissance and Pete Hamill. Later, in July 1975, Bob Marley and the Wailers recorded their breakthrough reggae album *Live!*, which included the classic 'No Woman No Cry'. At the end of October 1977, a 34-day tour of the UK, featuring artists on the Stiff Records label, had its climax at the Lyceum with a sell-out gig; among the performers were Ian Dury, Elvis Costello and Wreckless Eric. The Kinks wrote a tribute song called 'Come Dancing' about one of Ray Davies' six older sisters, Rene, and the Lyceum. Throughout her life she had suffered from heart problems. She died on Ray Davies' thirteenth birthday, while dancing on the ballroom floor. That same day Rene had given him his first guitar as a present.

During his tour of Britain in April 1965, Bob Dylan stayed at the Savoy Hotel. The location for the promo film of his song 'Subterranean Homesick Blues' was the road behind the hotel, Savoy Place. Featured in the classic documentary *Don't Look Back* by DA Pennebaker, the clip prefigured by years the pop videos that started with Queen's 'Bohemian Rhapsody' and later put MTV on the map. The hand-held captions, with statements like 'Think',

Above: The Clash appeared at venues all over London, playing to a loyal following. One of whom was Shane MacGowan (bottom right) seen here in 1977, at a local gig. At that time his own songwriting career was in the offing.

were written in his hotel room the previous night with the help of Donovan, himself touted as Britain's answer to Dylan. In November 1983, Mick Jagger stayed in Suite 312 of the Savoy while promoting the Stones' album *Undercover*. The wonderful Noel Coward was another regular guest at the Savoy Hotel.

In the mid 1970s, one of Ireland's greatest songwriters – no, not Bono, but Shane MacGowan of the Pogues – used to work behind the bar at the Griffin Inn, situated at 9 Villiers Street, at the Trafalgar Square end of the Strand.

HOLBORN

At 208-209 High Holborn is a big Victorian pub, the **Princess Louise**. It was the location for Ewan MacColl's influential Ballads and Blues folk club from 1954. An upper-floor room was one of the

Above: Oasis have gone from small gigs at the Water Rats pub to major, earth-trembling concerts at Wembley.

first venues in a expanding folk club movement. Ewan MacColl, father of the late singer Kirsty, and his wife Peggy Seeger were regular performers and visitors were encouraged to take part.

Rod Stewart made his TV debut in August 1964 on the ground-breaking pop programme *Ready Steady Go!*, filmed every Friday evening at the **Rediffusion Studios** (4-12 Kingsway) between autumn 1963 and spring 1965. After the show Rod Stewart met up with Ronnie Wood and would later form the Faces with him.

Firm proof that rock star girlfriends and managers rarely make great bedfellows in the world of rock'n'roll was provided at the recording of Jimi Hendrix's 'Hey Joe' in October 1966, at De Lane Lea Studios (129 Kingsway, now the offices of the Civil Aviation Authority). During the

recording Hendrix's girlfriend, Kathy Etchingham, walked in on a red light and Hendrix's manager, Chas Chandler, went ape. Interruptions aside, it was at these studios that the Jimi Hendrix Experience recorded together for the first time. Chandler was no stranger to the studios and was able to negotiate a special deal. In May 1964 his old band the Animals recorded their biggest hit, 'The House of the Rising Sun', here after touring with Chuck Berry. Legendary producer Mickie Most booked only a half-hour session and allowed them one take. The Rolling Stones recorded Lennon and McCartney's 'I Wanna Be Your Man' at the studios in October 1963.

Perhaps the most famous former student of the **London School of Economics** in Houghton Street was Mick Jagger. He attended the college in the early 1960s. Other ex-pupils include DJ Judge Jules and Matt Osman of Suede.

CHANCERY LANE

The long and winding legal battle that enveloped the Beatles' last years ended at the High Court near Chancery Lane. The final stop on their world tour was here in March 1971 when the band officially terminated. Paul McCartney split the group because he disagreed with manager Allen Klein's financial control. Years later in February 1988, Frankie Goes to Hollywood lead singer, Holly Johnson, defeated ZTT Records and Perfect Songs In the High Courts here. The company's injunction on his solo record contract with EMI was reversed. Johnson has been one of the few pop stars to prove successful in contractural disagreements with their record company. In the 1990s, Jason Donovan successfully sued *The Face* magazine after they alleged he was gay. He was awarded £500,000 in damages. But singer George Michael failed in his attempt to break his contract with Sony in the early 1990s and lost the same sum in court costs. The famous *Oz* obscenity trial took place here in January 1967. *Oz* was a hugely influential underground magazine of the 1960s, pioneered by Australian Richard Neville. In April 1970, John Lennon was cleared of the indecency charge relating to an exhibition (see Bond Street) he mounted of etchings, some depicting Yoko Ono in erotic poses, that was deemed to be indecent. The case was dismissed.

KING'S CROSS

In 1994, Oasis played their first headline gig at the **Water Rats**, 328 Grays Inn Road, which captured the attention of the music press. The pub leads something of a double life: during the day the Water Rats is a conventional King's Cross local full of office workers slagging off their

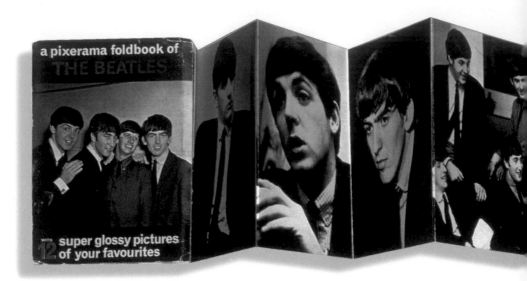

Above: The Beatles had a huge impact on the Swinging Sixties and today their music continues to influence bands such as Oasis.

bosses, but at 8 p.m. it becomes one of the most influential venues in the music business. Prior to 1985, the Water Rats was called the Pindar of Wakefield and a young and not-yet-famous Bob Dylan appeared in December 1962 in an early folk performance. Much later, in October 1982, the Pogues played their first gig here.

John Lydon, better known as Johnny Rotten, attended Kingsway College at 45 Sidmouth Street after leaving St William of York Roman Catholic Secondary School (opposite Pentonville Prison). In September 1973, Lydon met Jah Wobble (real name John Wardle) whilst enrolling at Kingsway. After the break-up of the Sex Pistols, Lydon teamed up with his old college mate to form Public Image Limited.

GOWER STREET

University College London on Gower Street boasts a glittering array of alumni. The band Coldplay met as undergraduate students at UCL, and they are just the latest in a long tradition of student band successes including Elastica, Suede and Basement Jaxx. Lloyd Cole also attended the college.

TOTTENHAM COURT ROAD

The Swinging Sixties saw rock'n'roll replace folky protest songs and tepid teeny bop, and ended with the rise of psychedelic clubs and the first signs of progressive rock. A venue called Rector's Club, at 31 Tottenham Court Road, was one of a select number of small London clubs

and restaurants that hosted jazz-flavoured dance music in the early 1920s. Four decades later, strange-looking aliens arrived and took over the place. They turned it into London's quintessential underground nightclub, the short-lived but hugely influential **UFO** club (see Chalk Farm). It took place on Friday nights, in the basement of an Irish pub, then called the Blarney Club, where the owner rented out the downstairs ballroom. Despite a short tenure, from December 1966 to October 1967, UFO quickly became Britain's first psychedelic club. Even the way you pronounced the name revealed just how tragically hip or hopelessly untrendy you were. It was pronounced 'U-FO' by those in the know, and 'U-F-O' by those who were not. Among the regular groups were the Move, Soft Machine (with a young Robert Wyatt) and Procol Harum. You might even have heard them play 'A Whiter Shade of Pale' here. However, it was Pink Floyd who became synonymous with the venue. Their reputation was established at the UFO club, and having made their mark, virtually became the house band. After the club's highly successful all-nighters, the hippy revellers, wearing bells on neck chains, would often straggle home at dawn, tinkling as they went. Ever-growing crowds and some negative drug reports in the Sunday newspapers forced the UFO club to move to the Roundhouse in Chalk Farm, in 1967. Like a bad trip, 31 Tottenham Court Road is gone but not forgotten. The whole block between Stephen Street and Percy Street was demolished to make way for, yes, you've guessed it, a row of hi-fi shops.

Acid casualty and UFO club icon Syd Barrett shared a bedsit for a number of months in Tottenham Street, off Tottenham Court Road, with his childhood friend David Gale. 'It was in a hideous block of deranged people and the rent tribunal practically insisted the landlord gave it to us for free it was so dreadful,' said Gale.

In February 1957, 32-year-old Bill Haley became the first American rock 'n' roller to appear in Britain when he debuted with his Comets at the **Dominion Theatre** (269 Tottenham Court Road). In September 1978, the showing of *Star Wars* was ditched in favour of seven consecutive nights of Elvis Costello and the Attractions concerts. German electronic-rockers Tangerine Dream were regulars, recording a live album here, although the venue has yet to host their still long-awaited *Unplugged* concert.

Right next door to the Dominion Theatre was a venue called the **Horseshoe Hotel**, 264–267 Tottenham Court Road, a pub which became a folk club in February 1967. Started by Bert Jansch and John Renbourn, the venue annoyed folk purists from the outset. As early as the first gig, the purely acoustic show was junked in favour of amplifiers, bass, drums and microphones.

In July 1968, on Mick Jagger's 25th birthday, a nightclub called the Vesuvio club – possibly named after the beatnik coffee house in San Francisco – was opened at 26 Tottenham Court Road. The club was jointly owned by Mick Jagger, Keith Richards and Tony Sanchez. Paul McCartney attended the opening party and made a big impression by playing an advance pressing of the Beatles' 'Hey Jude/Revolution'.

Sex Pistol Johnny Rotten once worked with Sid Vicious in Cranks restaurant at the top of Heals store, at 196 Tottenham Court Road. 'If only those health food hippies knew who was cleaning out their kitchen,' he said later. 'We cleaned it out in more ways than one. Night after night we stuffed our faces.'

NEW OXFORD STREET

The offices of Immediate Records, the label owned by the Rolling Stones' manager Andrew Loog Oldham, were located on New Oxford Street. Inaugurated in 1965, with its Stones connections and fresh attitude, Immediate was the hippest label a young band could hope to sign to. By the middle of 1966, the Small Faces felt they were in a straitjacket with a tough gig list and followed by hordes of screaming girls, but within a year all that changed when they moved to Immediate. They suddenly enjoyed creative freedom. Other early Immediate signings included Rod Stewart and PP Arnold, a former backing singer with Ike Turner.

Now a converted Muslim, Yusuf Islam, the singer formerly known as Cat Stevens, lived in a flat above his Greek Cypriot father's restaurant, the Moulin Rouge (49 New Oxford Street). Stevens attended a Roman Catholic School on Drury Lane and started gigging during a brief spell at Hammersmith College of Art.

In May 1964, Dick James moved his fast-growing empire of companies to nearby offices at 71–75 New Oxford Street. His company, **Dick James Music**, was the publishers of virtually every early Beatles' composition. James soon installed a recording studio at the back of the building in which the Beatles recorded in November 1966. The year before, Elton John and Bernie Taupin became staff writers for Dick James Music. They didn't actually meet until Elton

Opposite: Bill Haley and his Comets were the first American rock'n'rollers to play in Britain.

had written music to ten of Bernie's lyrics. In the late summer of 1967, Bernie turned up at the offices of Dick James Music where Elton was doing a piano overdub in the studio. Once Elton emerged they went off to the Lancaster Grill on Tottenham Court Road for coffee and talked non-stop about music. Dick James died in 1986 of a heart attack. Soon after, Elton John, Bernie Taupin and Elton's manager, John Reid, won a court case for unpaid royalties.

OXFORD STREET

Nowadays this charmless street feels rather like a shopping arcade that has yet to be pedestrianized. Still, all is not lost, as there are a number of memorable musical landmarks. Today it's hard to think of Elton John as skint, but back in 1967, during the recording of his first album *Empty Sky*, written with Bernie Taupin and produced by Steve Brown, he was flat broke. Often, Elton would finish work at 4 a.m. and walk to the Salvation Army Headquarters at 275 Oxford Street. Brown's father ran the place and lived above it. And it was here, over many nights, that Elton slept for a few hours on the sofa.

Below: From mohair to no hair, even in 2001 some punk bands are still appearing at the 100 Club on Oxford Street.

In July 1983, many years and best-selling albums later, Elton John met German recording engineer Renate Blauel at Air Studios. The premises were located at 214 Oxford Street and were owned by Beatles' producer George Martin. At the time, Elton was working on the final sessions for his *Too Low For Zero* album. The couple married in Australia on Valentine's Day the following year, with Elton's song-writing partner and lyricist, Bernie Taupin, as his best man. Many fans and observers wondered if the union was actually serious and the American magazine *People* succinctly pondered whether the new Mrs Elton John was 'a lover or a cover'. The couple divorced in 1988.

One of London's longest-running and most important live venues is also Oxford Street's most famous rock landmark. The legendary **100 Club**, named after its location at 100 Oxford Street, opened in October 1942 and still thrives today. It was originally named the

Feldman Swing Club, after jazz fan and budding clarinet player Robert Feldman took a break from his rag-trade job to manage the basement club. In 1950, it became the London Jazz Club, then the Humphrey Lyttelton Club (with Humph's band often in residence) and was also called Jazzshows. It finally became the 100 Club in 1964 and the name has remained. The club hosted an influential punk rock festival between 20–21 September 1976, featuring the Damned, the Clash, the Buzzcocks and headliners the Sex Pistols. It was also the occasion

Below: The 100 Club has seen it all from jazz to punk, and is still going strong.

100 CLUB
100 OXFORD ST.
Monday SEPTEMBER **20**
SEX PISTOLS
CLASH
SUB WAY SECT
SUZIE AND THE BANSHEES
AND FROM FRANCE
STINKY TOYS
OPEN 7 PM LATE BAR
ADMISSION £1.50
(£1.00 NUS ETC.)
7 PM LATE BAR

Above: What the late great Alexis Korner didn't know about blues probably wasn't worth knowing. His band Blues Inc helped put British R&B on the map.

for the first live performance by Siouxsie and the Banshees, with versatile Pistol Sid Vicious making his musical debut on drums. At another point in the festival, Sid hit out at legendary rock journalist Nick Kent with a bike chain and smashed a glass, blinding a member of the audience in the process. A few days later, the club was back to normal, featuring trad jazz regulars like George Melly and Ken Colyer's Jazzmen. This was typical of the 100 Club, which has always successfully straddled disparate musical styles. The punk tradition carries on with punk nights every Thursday. Punk band Alternative TV played at the venue in the summer of 2001.

Over the road was the nerve centre of Sex Pistols' manager Malcolm McLaren. On the first afternoon of the punk festival, the Pistols signed a contract with McLaren's company, **Glitterbest**, at 40 Dryden Chambers, 119 Oxford Street. In the same building was Miles Copeland, who managed the Police, several seedy tour operators and escort agencies as well as the offices of *Zigzag* magazine and *Sniffin' Glue* punk fanzine.

London's rich musical history would be a whole lot poorer without the world-famous Marquee club (see Charing Cross Road and Wardour Street). With three incarnations in nearly four decades, this was Soho's prime rock'n'roll venue. Its alumni reads like a who's who of twentieth-century popular music. The Marquee hosted them all and survived longer than most: psychedelics, punks, rock'n'rollers and metallers. All have been through its doors. Between 1958 and 1964, its original premises were at 165 Oxford Street, where London's best-known club name started life as a trad jazz hotspot in the basement of the Academy Picture House. It was called the Marquee Ballroom, with an interior designed by Angus McBean, complete with striped marquee-style awnings. McBean is better known to rock'n'roll almanacs and anoraks for photographing album covers featuring the Beatles leaning over the stairwell in the EMI headquarters. The first Marquee enjoyed plenty of links with the early days of the Rolling Stones. In March 1962, Brian Jones saw legendary bluesman Muddy Waters perform live here. And the next day, inspired by the gig, he put an advert in *Jazz News* looking for musicians to join his rhythm and blues band. The band was originally named the Rollin' Stones after a 1950 Muddy Waters' song. Four months later in July 1962, with Mick Jagger and Keith Richards on board, the group played its first gig at the Marquee as an interval act for Alexis Korner's Blues Incorporated. Later in January 1964, Rod Stewart made his professional singing debut at the Marquee with Long John Baldry and the Hoochie Coochie Men.

Whichever way you look at it, the career of the Beatles began in earnest in early 1962, further down the road, in offices above the **HMV** Shop at 363 Oxford Street (see map on p65). HMV's flagship store was opened in 1921 by Edward Elgar and it was here that the demo tape from the band's failed Decca audition was first heard by George Martin. The tape had been recommended to the legendary producer by an engineer at Decca and Martin was sufficiently excited to sign them to EMI without a formal try-out. The rest is history.

MARGARET STREET

An after-hours basement for jamming just north of Soho, the **Speakeasy** club was at 48 Margaret Street. Soon after it opened in January 1967, the Speakeasy became the epicentre

> One night at the Speakeasy, Jimi had gone on stage leaving his Scotch and Coke at our table. Without thinking I sipped at Jimi's drink while he played. I began to imagine I could actually see the music going around the room and it was becoming unbearably loud until I thought my eardrums would explode. I noticed that the faces of the people around me were moving and distorting horribly and I began to become very afraid.

FRIEND OF HENDRIX

for London's beautiful people and rock'n'roll elite. Many good bands played here but gaining entrance was a problem. It was the 'in place' to go and entry seemed to be reserved for those with at least one current hit in the charts. All the guests seemed to know each other and there were no VIP areas or security guards. The Speakeasy lasted longer than most clubs, witnessing the most exciting times in British pop music: the late 1960s and the mid-1970s. A wreathed coffin served as the reception desk and the interior was initially designed to match its American prohibition theme. Later, it was decorated in orange, green and pink, in the style of an Indian pavilion. The Speakeasy quickly became the place where the prime movers in the music industry and musicians went after hours. It featured all-star jams the likes of which are unthinkable nowadays. Eric Clapton often played and the club was frequently visited by the Beatles. Jimi Hendrix played some early gigs here and on one occasion even jammed with Jane Asher's mother, who was a violinist and a professor at London's Guildhall School of Music.

According to Kathy Etchingham in her book about her former boyfriend, Jimi Hendrix, and the 1960s there was one young guest who always sat at a table inside the door of the Speakeasy, studying the stars as they came and went. 'He was noticeable because of his extraordinarily long black hair. Guests used to make jokes about him because he looked a bit of a geek, but no one spoke to him or knew anything about him. Years later, he became famous as Freddie Mercury.' Deep Purple played their first gig here in 1969, while Thin Lizzy's English debut took place the following year. Later, the New York Dolls' drummer, Billy Murcia, spent his last night at the club, dying

Right: The Speakeasy, with its coffin in reception and lurid wallpaper, was one of the most hip places to go and be seen during the 1960s and 1970s.

in early November 1972 of, yes, you've guessed it, drug abuse. David Bowie's 'Time' suggested his demise involved a quantity of Quaalude sedatives and red wine. Bowie himself was no stranger to the club. At the launch party of progressive rockers King Crimson in April 1969, Bowie met an American design student called Angie Barnett and they married the following year. The couple divorced in 1980. When Pete Townshend famously met the Sex Pistols at the club, he told them they were the only hope for rock.

The Who's drummer Keith Moon spent the last evening of his life at a party held at what is now a pub-cum-wine bar in Upper St Martin's Lane. It was 7 September 1978 and the occasion was a Buddy Holly convention organized by Paul McCartney. Moon died later at his girlfriend's flat in Mayfair.

When the Beatles moved down to London in 1963, Paul McCartney lodged at the central London home of the parents of his girlfriend, aspiring actress Jane Asher. For three years McCartney lived at **57 Wimpole Street** in the spare attic bedroom at the back of the house. Whilst living here he wrote 'I Wanna Hold Your Hand' for Jane Asher and 'Yesterday'. In 1965, McCartney bought his own house in Cavendish Avenue, very handy indeed for Abbey Road Studios, thank-you-very-much.

EUSTON ROAD

One of the most memorable incidents in television's glorious history took place in Studio 5 at **Thames TV**'s headquarters on the Euston Road. The Sex Pistols caused national outrage on 1 December 1976 when they appeared (plus gathered friends including Siouxsie Sioux) on the *Today* show with Bill Grundy. Freddie Mercury and Queen were originally due to appear, but the Pistols filled in at the last minute. The interview culminated in guitarist Steve Jones calling the grumpy Grundy, a 'dirty fucker', amongst other things, on live television. Classic TV in retrospect, but the following morning, the shockwaves reverberated round the UK as grandmothers up and down the country choked on their cornflakes reading about Johnny Rotten and his pals. The tabloids had a field day and the Sex Pistols were proclaimed Public Enemy Number One. McLaren's men were hurled into the headlines and within days the whole country knew about punk and, once again, popular culture had been reinvented. Grundy simply hadn't been able to

Ke y		
❶ Thames TV	❾ EMI House	⓲ Heddon Street
❷ Royal Academy of Music	❿ 34 Montagu Square	⓳ Sybilla's
❸ Ivor Court	⓫ 13a Bryanstone Mews East	⓴ Mason's Yard
❹ 25 Hanover Gate Mansions	⓬ Cumberland Hotel	㉑ Liberty Records
❺ Marylebone Magistrates Court	⓭ Pye Recording Studios	㉒ Ritz
❻ Apple Boutique	⓮ HMV	㉓ White Elephant
❼ 57 Wimpole Street	⓯ 23 Brook Street	㉔ Radio London
❽ IBC Studios	⓰ London Arts Gallery	㉕ 9 Curzon Place
	⓱ Apple Corporation	㉖ Hilton International Hotel

Marylebone, Marble Arch, Piccadilly & Mayfair

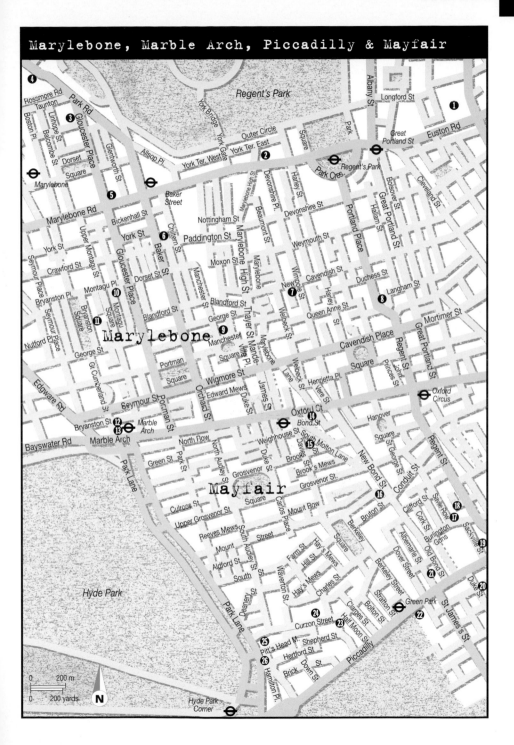

Regent's Park

Rossmore Rd
Taunton
Park Rd
Boston Pl
Linhope St
Gloucester Place
Balcombe St
Dorset
Square
Marylebone
Glentworth St
Allsop Pl

Albany St
Longford St
Euston Rd
Great
Portland St
Regent's Park
Park
York Bridge
York Gate
Outer Circle
York Ter. East
York Ter. West
Square
Park Cres.
Boscoe St
Cleveland St
Great Portland St
Harley St
Devonshire Pl
Devonshire St
Portland Place
Hallam St
Baker
Street
Bickenhall St
Nottingham St
Beaumont St
Weymouth St
Duchess St
Langham St
York St
Chiltern St
Paddington St
Marylebone High St
Moxon St
Wimpole St
Cavendish St
Queen Anne St
Mortimer St
Upper Montagu St
Baker St
Dorset St
Blandford St
George St
Thayer St
Mandeville Pl
Welbeck St
Wigmore St
Henrietta Pl
Cavendish Place
Great Portland St
Regent St
John Princes St
Oxford
Circus
York St
Crawford St
Montagu Pl
Blandford St
Manchester St
Manchester
Square
Seymour Place
Bryanston Pl
Seymour St
Wimpole St
Welbeck St
Marylebone Lane
James St
Nutford Place
George St
Gt. Cumberland St
Portman
Square
Edward Mews
Duke St
Oxford St
Bond St
Hanover
Square
New Bond St
St George St
Conduit St
Regent St
Edgware Rd
Bryanston St
Marble
Arch
North Row
North Audley St
Weighhouse St
South Molton Lane
Bayswater Rd
Marble Arch
Green St
North Row
Duke St
Brook St
Brook's Mews
Clifford St
Cork St
Burlington Gdns
Sackville St
Bruton St
Savile Row
Old Bond St
Grosvenor St
Grosvenor St
Berkeley St
Albemarle St
Duke St
Park Lane
Park Lane
Cultross St
Upper Grosvenor St
Grosvenor
Square
Carlos Place
Mount Row
Reeves Mews
South Audley St
Mount
Street
Aldford St
South
Farm St
Hill St
Hay's Mews
Charles St
Waverton St
Hay's Mews
Charles St
Berkeley Square
Dover Street
Berkeley Street
Stratton St
Old Bond St
Duke St
St. James's St

Marylebone

Mayfair

Hyde Park

Clarges St
Hall Moon St
Green Park
Curzon Street
Pitt's Head M.
Shepherd St
Hertford St
Brick St
Down St
Hamilton Pl
Bolton St
Piccadilly

Hyde Park
Corner

0   200 m
0   200 yards
N

keep his dislike of the band to himself and the interview resulted in his sacking. Thames TV moved out of Euston Road when they lost their ITV licence at the end of 1992 and are now situated at their studio complex in Teddington.

A week before their memorable performance at the 1985 Live Aid concert at Wembley Stadium, Queen rehearsed for three days at the **Shaw Theatre** on the Euston Road. While other artists turned up and busked it on the day, Queen's hard work paid off and their 18-minute medley of hits easily stole the Wembley show. This was despite Freddie Mercury suffering from a bad cold and being told by doctors he was too ill to perform.

MARYLEBONE

Marylebone Magistrates Court, once at 181 Marylebone Road, was closed in 1998 after 200 years of service and it's unlikely many rock'n'roll visionaries mourned its passing. Sid Vicious and his girlfriend Nancy Spungeon appeared here on amphetamine charges in May 1978. Back in November 1968, John Lennon and Yoko Ono appeared in court charged with possession of one ounce of cannabis resin at their flat (see Montagu Square). Yoko was acquitted, but Lennon pleaded guilty and was fined £150. The US Immigration and Naturalization Service later denied Lennon the right to live in America due to this 1968 conviction. Marylebone's roll of honour also includes Keith Richards (1973) and Jimmy Page (1984) both on drug-related charges.

Although most of the Beatles' first film, *A Hard Day's Night*, was shot at Twickenham film studios, one sequence was filmed at Paddington Station. For the opening scenes of the movie the Fab Four boarded the train at Acton main line station. These scenes were shot on two consecutive Sundays at Marylebone Station (Great Central Street) in April 1964. The screaming, rampaging hordes of teenagers were actually real Beatles' fans who discovered the film location and were trying to get closer to their idols. The famous opening shot in *A Hard Day's Night*, which shows John, George, Ringo and Paul running, was filmed near the station in Boston Place. George Harrison's trip and fall was an accident and not in the script.

Since its foundation in 1822, Britain's top musical conservatory, the **Royal Academy of Music**, on Marylebone Road, has produced classical musicians and even a few rock stars, including musical virtuoso John Cale, Elton John, Joe Jackson, David Palmer of Jethro Tull and Annie Lennox of the Eurythmics, who won a scholarship in 1971 aged 17. Back in 1958, Elton won a scholarship and attended classes every Saturday. He was honoured with a Fellowship of the Academy in 1997.

In the late 1950s, Cliff Richard shared a flat in Cecil House, at 99–100 Marylebone High Street. At the time, he was only just breaking into London's music scene with his backing group, the Shadows.

At 35 Portland Place, some classic songs were recorded in the basement of the former **IBC Studios**. The Who recorded 'My Generation' here and the Kinks recorded their classic first no. 1, 'You Really Got Me', in July 1964. They were accompanied by two session players, future Led Zeppelin founder Jimmy Page on guitar and Deep Purple's Jon Lord on Hammond organ. Some early Rolling Stones recordings took place here in 1963.

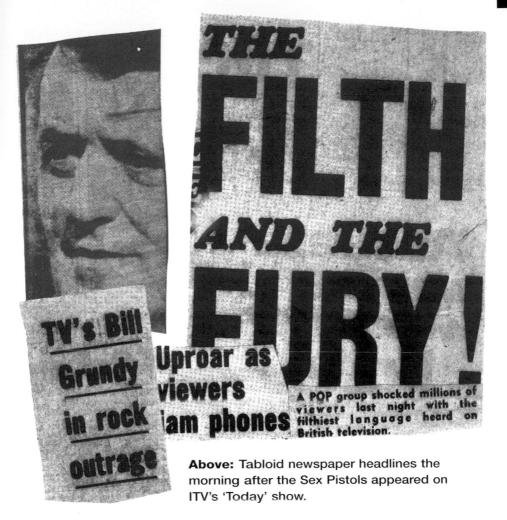

Above: Tabloid newspaper headlines the morning after the Sex Pistols appeared on ITV's 'Today' show.

In January 1967, Yoko Ono and her then husband, Tony Cox, moved into **25 Hanover Gate Mansions** on Park Road, opposite Kent Passage. She lived in this block of flats until John Lennon came on the scene and in July 1968 she moved with him into Ringo Starr's flat (see Montagu Square).

BAKER STREET

You don't have to be Sherlock Holmes to locate the former premises of the Beatles' shop, the **Apple Boutique**. Put away the magnifying glass because it's not there any more. It was situated at 94 Baker Street (at the junction of Baker Street and Paddington Street) and is now an employment agency called Let It Be. The original idea for the shop came about in 1967 when the Beatles were advised by their accountants that if they didn't put money into a business they would have to cough up millions of pounds in tax. From its opening in December 1967 until the end of July the following year, it was a hugely popular place to shop. Originally, its outside walls were decorated with huge colourful murals but these were later painted over in more sober shades when the neighbouring shop took them to court. Apple Corps planned to open further fashion ventures in Liverpool, Birmingham and Manchester but these came to nothing. Although massively popular with the public, the boutique was forced to close after just seven months due to bad management and financial chaos.

In the early 1960s it seemed you couldn't manage a band unless you operated out of **Ivor Court** at the top of Gloucester Place, off Baker Street. In 1963, Andrew Loog Oldham, the fashionable, first manager of the Rolling Stones, formed the group's management offices at his flat, 138 Ivor Court. In the autumn of 1964, the Who's management team of Kit Lambert and Chris Stamp (younger brother of actor Terence) worked out of Lambert's flat at 113. Sixties popsters Herman's Hermits also lived in a flat in Ivor Court.

Another regular haunt for pop stars, Marylebone Register Office (now Westminster Register Office) in Gloucester Place was the place to tie the knot if you were in the Beatles, or wanted to be. Paul McCartney and Linda Eastman married here in March 1969, when crowds of well-wishers were so large that the couple had to enter the registry office from the rear alley, passing the rubbish bins *en route*. Some 12 years later, in April 1981, Ringo Starr wed actress Barbara Bach; both Beatles' ceremonies were officiated over by the same registrar, Joseph Jevans. Ringo's wedding was the first time the remaining Beatles appeared together in public following the murder of John Lennon in New York four months earlier. Much later, in April 1997, Liam Gallagher of Oasis married actress and singer Patsy Kensit here, after their February wedding had been postponed. The marriage didn't last.

Angus McBean's famous photographs of the Beatles leaning over the stairwell were taken in the record company headquarters at **EMI House**, 20 Manchester Square. The Fabs visited the building on many occasions, recording radio shows and performing live. The building is best known for the covers of 'Please Please Me' and their first two compilation albums. McBean snapped the Beatles looking over the railing down from the first floor to the entrance of the building. He took the first photograph in February 1963 and returned in May 1969 to shoot them in precisely the same location. By then, however, their faces were more hirsute, the clothes more free-spirited and they looked like IRA hunger-strikers on a tea break. Brit poppers Blur were photographed in exactly the same pose in August 1995, the same month as EMI moved from Manchester Square to Brook Green near Hammersmith.

MONTAGU SQUARE

It's not quite Abbey Road Studios, but Beatles pilgrims still visit a townhouse in a smart square near Marble Arch which has plenty of band connections. Ringo Starr was the first Beatle to live at the ground floor and basement flat at **34 Montagu Square**. He bought the flat in early 1965, living here for a short time before renting it out. Meanwhile he married Maureen Cox and moved to a country house called 'Sunny Heights' in Weybridge. Ringo's first tenant was Paul McCartney who turned the flat into a mini-recording studio and wrote several Beatles songs, including 'Eleanor Rigby', in the basement. Next Jimi Hendrix rented the flat with his manager, Chas Chandler, in

Above: The Apple boutique in Baker Street circa 1968. Although popular it closed after only seven months.

December, but four months later Starr evicted the pair after they painted all the rooms black. Later, in July 1968, Ringo let the flat to John Lennon and Yoko Ono after the singer left his wife Cynthia, son Julian and their Weybridge home. The flat in Montagu Square was John and Yoko's first place as a couple, and it was here that the couple shot the controversial album cover for *Two Virgins*. Apple employee Tony Bramwell set up the camera for them and rushed away before any clothes were shed. EMI refused to touch the record and it was left to a smaller independent label to distribute it. In October 1968, police raided the flat and discovered a small quantity of cannabis resin. Lennon and Yoko were arrested and John was subsequently convicted (see Marylebone Road). The arrest later had serious implications for Lennon's application for US citizenship. Ringo Starr sold the flat in February 1969 after more than his fair share of tenant problems.

MARBLE ARCH

Inevitably rock'n'roll deaths tend to be somewhat romanticized and the more untimely the death the bigger the legend. Trouble is, the locales of these deaths are often less than romantic. Jimi Hendrix died in rooms 507–508 of the **Cumberland Hotel** in Great Cumberland Place, near Marble Arch on 18 September 1970. His girlfriend, Monika Dannemann, couldn't rouse him so she called an ambulance. He was pronounced dead upon arrival at St Mary's Hospital, Paddington. Hendrix died from choking on his own vomit, caused by an overdose of drugs taken earlier in the day at Dannemann's basement flat (see Notting Hill). Dannemann herself committed suicide in 1996 after losing a court case. It had been known for some months that Hendrix had been in an increasingly bad way due to his escalating intake of drugs.

Until his death few drugs-related deaths had affected the rock business. Hendrix's death shook an industry that, apart from Brian Jones's early demise, had yet to experience much of a toll. Predictably, the media were gleeful. In her excellent book, former girlfriend Kathy Etchingham said it was just the sort of end they wished on a man like Jimi, who flouted all the rules of social behaviour. It was like the final chapter of a cautionary tale for children.

The Kinks' first official recording session took place at **Pye Recording Studios**, 40 Bryanston Street, near Marble Arch, in January 1964. They recorded the Little Richard song 'Long Tall Sally'. Pye agreed to release the record on their label if the Kinks, still called the Bo Weevils after a song by Bo Diddley, paid their own recording costs. The band were still to enjoy a brief spell as the Ravens (named after the Vincent Price horror film) before settling on the Kinks. Eventually, they got the name that stuck because of the kinky boots that band members wore, similar to those seen on Honor Blackman in *The Avengers*. 'And because our new drummer looked like a police identikit of a pervert, we might as well call ourselves the Kinks,' recalled Dave Davies. The Who's 'I Can't Explain' was also recorded here.

In the spring of 1965, Mick Jagger moved into a small mews house at **13a Bryanston Mews East**, to live alone for the first time. He had spent a couple of years living in flats and houses with the other Stones and craved a bit of space. He stayed here for almost a year, moving out in early 1966.

By 1971, Marc Bolan's success allowed him to move to 47 Bilton Towers, Great Cumberland Place, overlooking Hyde Park.

PARK LANE

In late August 1965, the Rolling Stones met Allen Klein for the first time at the **Hilton International Hotel**, 22 Park Lane. Within just a few days he became their financial manager, leaving Andrew Oldham to take care of personal management. Several years after leaving Pink Floyd, Syd Barrett lived in a penthouse suite here, between 1972–74. Hefty royalties from the group's early albums guaranteed Barrett didn't starve. In late July 1977, Elvis Costello performed an impromptu gig outside the hotel. CBS Records was holding its annual

Below: Guitar legend Jimi Hendrix in 1970. That same year he succumbed to his rock 'n' roll lifestyle.

international conference and Costello shamelessly wanted to plug his gig that night at Dingwalls in Camden Lock. A crowd gathered, including several senior CBS executives, and a tourist who asked for a Neil Diamond song. As so often is the case, neither police nor hotel management saw the funny side and Costello was promptly arrested. As a publicity stunt it worked. Costello and his band the Attractions were signed by CBS before the end of the year.

PICCADILLY

When Paul McCartney married New York photographer Linda Eastman in March 1969, they held their wedding reception at the famous **Ritz** Hotel, 150-153 Piccadilly. Among the guests were fellow Beatle George Harrison and his wife, model Pattie Boyd. Eric Clapton later wrote 'Layla' about Boyd after falling in love with her. Mick Jagger stayed at this top hotel between December 1978 and January 1979, penning 'Start Me Up', the first single from the Stones' 1981 album, *Tattoo You*. Jagger stayed at the Ritz during his tax-exile-on-main-street years when he wasn't permitted to reside at his Cheyne Walk residence.

In March 1972, Roxy Music recorded the sound of a motorbike going up and down Piccadilly for their distinctive song, 'Virginia Plain'. Roxy were recording their debut album at 201 Piccadilly, the former premises of Command Studios. The studios were once the BBC's Piccadilly Studios, the site of many recordings by the Beatles for the Beeb.

The London Pavilion, at 3 Piccadilly Circus, first opened as a music-hall theatre in 1885, becoming a

major West End cinema as early as 1934. Scenes of uncontrollable Beatlemania enveloped the venue and much of the surrounding area when the Beatles' films, *A Hard Day's Night*, *Help* and *Yellow Submarine*, were premiered here in the 1960s. All four Fabs were always in attendance. However, none of them turned up here for the premiere of their fourth and final movie, *Let It Be*, in May 1970. Since 1989, the former London Pavilion has housed Rock Circus on the top floor and a Madame Tussaud's

Above: Elvis Costello and the Attractions in early poses.

exhibition of rock'n'roll wax models, including influential artists such as the Beatles, Jimi Hendrix and Bucks Fizz, er, just kidding on that last one.

CURZON STREET

Ringo Starr arrived at the former offices of pirate radio station **Radio London**, 17 Curzon Street, at the end of July 1967 to record a farewell message from the Beatles. It was broadcast on the station's last day on air. Nearby, the **White Elephant** restaurant and nightclub, at 28 Curzon Street, had been a favourite nocturnal haunt of the Beatles in the 1960s.

ALBEMARLE STREET

In 1967, Elton John met songwriting partner Bernie Taupin for the first time, through the former **Liberty Records**, a licenced label of EMI at 11 Albemarle Street. Liberty were an American record label and Elton John replied to their advertisement for recording artists. At the time he was frustrated doing mostly session work and playing with Long John Baldry in his band Bluesology. Desperately wanting a solo career, Elton auditioned but failed to win a record deal. However, all was not lost as Liberty gave him some lyrics sent to them by Taupin. Elton corresponded with Taupin by letter for several months before eventually meeting him.

MAYFAIR

Only one locale in London has the remarkable and rather unfortunate distinction of hosting not one but two rock'n'roll deaths – **9 Curzon Place** in Mayfair. (Mama) Cass Elliot, former singer with the Mamas and the Papas died in flat 12, in this serviced block, in July 1974, after two sell-out concerts at the London Palladium. At the time the flat was owned by the singer Harry Nilsson. Rumours circulated that the 32-year-old Cass had choked on a ham sandwich, but an autopsy revealed a heart attack brought on by obesity and that old chestnut, excessive drug use. Four years later, in a cruel twist of fate, Keith Moon, the drummer with the Who, was found dead in the same place. He was discovered by his Swedish model girlfriend, Annette Walter-Lax. He had spent the previous evening with Paul and Linda McCartney at a Buddy Holly convention party in central London. Moon, also aged 32, died after watching the film *The Abominable Doctor Phibes*, starring Vincent Price. Unable to sleep, Moon took an overdose of his prescribed Heminevrin pills; ironically, they were drugs he was taking to fight his alcoholism. This central London flat was a modest abode compared to his space-age house in Chertsey which he'd sold to ex-10cc member Kevin Godley in 1974. There he'd cemented his nickname Moon the Loon by ordering a helicopter to fly him to the pub at the end of his driveway and driving his Rolls Royce into his swimming pool. Oasis visualized this image to good effect on the cover of their album *Be Here Now*.

Predictably, a block of offices occupy 14 Berkeley Street, the site of the former Blue Angel nightclub, a regular mid-1960s after hours watering-hole for the Beatles. At 14–16 Bruton Place is the former site of Le Prince, a club which housed a discotheque called the Revolution Club. This venue was regularly played by Cream and was a favoured hangout for Eric Clapton in the late 1960s.

BOND STREET

'They smelt of pubs, and Wormwood Scrubs and too many right-wing meetings'. It seemed obvious, early on, that Paul

Above: Keith Moon's last night on earth with his Swedish girlfriend at a Buddy Holly convention party. In a perverse irony he died from an overdose of pills designed to combat his alcoholism.

Weller's lyrics would last far longer than his first band the Jam. The trio from Woking were photographed for the cover of the 'Down In The Tube Station At Midnight' single on a platform at **Bond Street underground station**.

Long before punk, in 1970, 'Bag One', John Lennon's exhibition of erotic lithographs of Yoko Ono, at the **London Arts Gallery**, 22 Bond Street, was closed by the police. Eight of the prints were confiscated as evidence of pornography. A court case ensued (see Chancery Lane), during which examples of Picasso's work were cited and the charges dropped.

Above: Hendrix was born in Seattle, but died and was honoured in London.

BROOK STREET

At **23 Brook Street** in Mayfair, an English Heritage blue plaque marks the flat where Jimi Hendrix lived in the late 1960s with his girlfriend, Kathy Etchingham. They lived above a restaurant called Mr Love, now even more fittingly an upmarket underwear shop. At the time of writing, plans are afoot to open a museum above the flat. The Seattle-born rock icon is in good company; another blue plaque next door commemorates the German composer George Handel, who lived at 25 Brook Street, albeit more than two centuries earlier. Now, Handel is not quite rock'n'roll, sure, but he had more in common with Hendrix than you might think. Both fled their native lands to find recognition and build international careers. Hendrix's blue plaque is a milestone in a number of ways. He was the first rock star to be honoured by English Heritage, and the first black man to receive such a distinction. Its unveiling came with opposition from some stuffy quarters who believed that in honouring a rock star English Heritage was degrading and dumbing down their blue plaque tradition. Hendrix had only been in Britain for four years when he died and received the honour in London rather than Seattle because it was here that he made his mark.

REGENT STREET

Just off Regent Street, at 3 Savile Row, was the former early nineteenth-century residence of Admiral Lord Nelson and his mistress Lady Hamilton. At one stage it was also a gambling den. For music fans, the building is far better known as the headquarters of the Beatles' **Apple Corporation** – or Apple Corps (Apple Core, geddit?). Soon after the Beatles moved to the premises in 1968, fans, who were nicknamed Apple Scruffs, camped out permanently on the doorstep outside, hoping to catch a glimpse of one or more of their heroes. All five floors of the building were carpeted in apple green, and until the mid-1970s, the apple-white, oak front door was covered with what was probably the most graffiti in history. Every millimetre was decorated with messages from Beatles' fans from all over the world and Ringo Starr later featured a photograph of the door on the cover of his 1976 album, *Ringo's Rotogravure*. When the door was finally removed, it was reportedly shipped to John Lennon and Yoko Ono's apartment in the Dakota building in New York. A replacement door received the same treatment, but only for a short while, as the Apple Corporation moved out in October 1976.

Now, unromantically, the building houses the head offices of the Building Societies Association. The Apple Building was the site of the Beatles' famous, unannounced, rooftop concert at lunchtime on 30 January 1969. The impromptu live performance was the last time they ever played to an audience. The concert brought traffic on all the neighbouring streets to a standstill until the Royal Bank of Scotland opposite complained and police constables from nearby police stations stopped the concert just 40 minutes later. The last song the Beatles ever played live was 'Get Back'.

An early version of Pink Floyd was formed in 1963 when Roger Waters met Nick Mason and Richard Wright when they were all architecture students at the Regent Street Polytechnic (now the University of Westminster) at 309 Regent Street. They formed a band called Sigma 6, but Pink Floyd proper came about when Syd Barrett, an old friend of Waters from

Below: 'Thank you on behalf of the group and ourselves, and I hope we've passed the audition.' John Lennon speaks for the Beatles on the roof of the Apple Building in January 1969.

Cambridge, joined. They played gigs at the poly in autumn 1964 and spring 1965. 'I was a middle-class student until we turned professional and then the business of the day-to-day running of a band, it's a bit like running a corner shop,' Pink Floyd drummer Nick Mason told *Mojo* magazine. Jimi Hendrix made a real impression here on 1 October 1966, when he jammed with Eric Clapton and Cream. Hendrix had recently arrived in London, brought over to the UK by former Animals' bassist Chas Chandler. The then-unknown American guitar virtuoso subsequently blew Clapton off-stage with a version of Howlin' Wolf's 'Killing Floor'. Clapton later admitted he was 'unprepared'.

You wouldn't know from the photographs, but David Bowie was suffering from flu when he posed for the album cover of *Ziggy Stardust* (*The Rise and Fall of Ziggy Stardust and the Spiders From Mars* for those Bowie pedants) in **Heddon Street**, off Regent Street. The shots were taken one night in January 1972 and the wet and cold weather conditions can't have helped Bowie's illness much. Photographer Brian Ward shot 17 black-and-white photos, including those used for the colourized front and back album covers. Seven photographs were taken of Bowie posing in front of 23 Heddon Street and four in and around the Heddon Street phone booth. Another six were close-up photographs of Bowie in the doorway and under a street-light.

Bowie's fifth album charted the story of Ziggy Stardust in eleven songs (including the well-known 'Suffragette City' and 'Starman'), his rise to stardom and consequent ruin. The Ziggy live concerts that followed pleasured fans, but also attracted press interest when Bowie simulated fellatio on Mick Ronson during the guitarist's lengthy improvised solos. Bowie killed off Ziggy at the end of his 1973 tour. With his anticipated replacement, Aladdin Sane – covered in white greasepaint except for a blue and red lightning flash across his face – Bowie once again successfully reinvented himself.

SWALLOW STREET

All four Beatles attended a private launch party on 22 June 1966 for the opening of **Sybilla's**, a fashionable London nightclub at 9 Swallow Street. Part-financed by George Harrison and run by Terry Howard, the club was one of London's nocturnal in-places until it closed in August 1968. Since its 1915 opening as the Studio club, the basement of this building has always housed nightclubs. Currently it is a club called The Opal Lounge.

MASON'S YARD

Just south of Piccadilly, hidden away in **Mason's Yard**, was the art gallery where John Lennon first met Yoko Ono in November 1966. Lennon had made it known that he was a possible financial backer for Yoko's conceptual art works so she invited him to a sneak preview of her nine-day exhibition 'Unfinished Objects and Paintings', at the Indica Gallery, 6 Mason's Yard. The gallery, owned by Barry Miles, Peter Asher and John Dunbar (Marianne Faithfull's first husband) was dedicated to the burgeoning contemporary/underground literature and art scene in London. When Lennon arrived Yoko gave him a scrap of paper with 'Breathe' scribbled on it.

As a 16-year-old in 1963, the influential rock photographer Gered Mankowitz had a first floor studio in the building next to the Indica Gallery. He captured everyone from Jimi Hendrix and the Small Faces to Kate Bush, Eric Clapton, the Verve and Oasis. He is best known for his photographs of the Rolling Stones, taken at the peak of their success, looking innocent and waiting to be corrupted, not yet eclipsed by the excess of indulgence and fame. Aged 17, Mankowitz also shot Marianne Faithfull for Stones' manager, Andrew Oldham. A year later, the manager commissioned the album cover for the Rolling Stones' *Out of Our Heads* and Mankowitz asked to join them on their US tour in 1965. His studio was a hip hangout. Painted brown and white with orange water pipes, there was a blown-up comic image of Batman on the landing with a bubble coming out of his mouth saying, 'It's as well to remember that evil is a pretty bad thing.' Rock stars of the day often called in to see him *en route* to the near-by Scotch of St James. 'Hendrix would always pop into the studio for a smoke on his way to the Scotch,' said the photographer. 'We'd chat, gossip. I liked him a lot. He had no side to him, no hidden agenda. He was a good guy.'

A few doors away in this hemmed-in court-yard behind St James Square was no. 13 Mason's Yard, the Scotch of St James. It opened in March 1965 and was a hugely popular Swinging Sixties nightclub and live music venue. The Scotch, as it was affectionately known, was one of the hippest clubs of the time and was frequented by anyone who aspired to be incredibly fashionable and those who'd already made it. It wasn't called the Scotch for nothing; it had outlandish Scottish baronial decor – plaid lampshades, bagpipes on the wall and even the waiters wore tartan waistcoats.

The Beatles were treated like royalty when they visited. They had their own table fitted with a brass plate bearing their name. In February 1966, Paul McCartney attended a gig by Stevie Wonder here and after the show the two met and formed a long-lasting friendship. Fifteen years later the duo collaborated on a couple of songs for McCartney's album *Tug of War*, including 'Ebony and Ivory', a single most would agree was neither artist's greatest musical moment.

Almost the minute Jimi Hendrix arrived in London in September 1966, chaperoned by Chas Chandler, he had his first jam and mesmerized the Scotch audience with his guitar antics. Chandler had to force Hendrix off the stage because he only had a seven-day visitor's visa and he was not supposed to be working.

> *Jimi got up and jammed. Kit and I could see this guy was something special and we wanted to get involved. We checked it out and found he had a manager, we couldn't produce him, so the only thing left was a record deal.*
>
> CHRIS STAMP ON SEEING HENDRIX PLAY AT THE SCOTCH

NORTH WEST

Every day visitors head to London's most famous rock landmark, the Abbey Road Studios and zebra crossing. Not too far away is Primrose Hill where the Rolling Stones were photographed for one of their album covers. Nearby Camden Town, North London's very own Soho, is the home of local nutty boys, Madness, and a whole lotta venues; The Electric Ballroom, Chalk Farm's Roundhouse and the Dublin Castle, where up-and-coming bands play today. Further out, venues don't come bigger than Wembley Stadium; there's also Harrow where the Who were discovered and Pinner, birthplace of Elton John.

Greasy Truckers
'Live at Dingwall's Dancehall'

Camel ✪ Gong ✪ Henry Cow ✪ Global Village Trucking Co.

Dingwalls Dance Hall at Camden Lock was opened in 1973.

The venue catered for all kinds of musical tastes.

CAMDEN

Camden Town was in effect the Soho of the late 1970s and one of its most exciting venues was the **Electric Ballroom**, opening at 184 Camden High Street in the summer of 1978. The site started life as an Irish ballroom in the 1930s, originally featuring showbands catering for large numbers of Irish immigrants who lived in Camden. It wasn't until much later that it became a major rock venue attracting most of the big bands. Some of the hottest acts of the past few decades have played here, including local nutty boys Madness, the Sex Pistols, Elastica and Moby. It was an important venue during the punk era and Sid Vicious performed his last UK gig here in August 1978, before he left for the US. The concert was called 'Sid Sods Off' and Glen Matlock, replaced in the Pistols by Vicious, was a member of his band. The following September, Adam and the Ants played two sell-out shows here. The Electric Ballroom is still going today, but its future is uncertain at the time of writing, because of ambitious London Underground plans to build a bigger station at Camden Town. These plans involve bulldozing the Electric Ballroom for a new station concourse, and they are being strongly resisted by those at the Ballroom and of course its legion of fans.

A rock'n'roll lifestyle is hardly conducive to good health and longevity. An endless supply of drugs, cash and fast women, often combined with egos the size of the Albert Hall, can be a deadly cocktail. As a result many rock stars have met their maker in London. Bon Scott, the former lead singer of Australian rock band AC/DC, died in 1980 after a touch too much to drink at the **Music Machine**, 1a Camden High Street, known as the **Camden Palace** since 1982. This huge venue first opened in 1900 as the Camden Theatre and hosted variety acts throughout the 1920s before becoming a BBC TV studio during the 1950s and 1960s, where 'The Goons' was recorded. In May 1977, when the Music Machine opened, Siouxie and the Banshees and ex-New York Doll Johnny Thunders and his band the Heartbreakers were among the first acts to play. Andy Summers, Sting and Stewart Copeland first played

Camden, Kentish Town & Primrose Hill

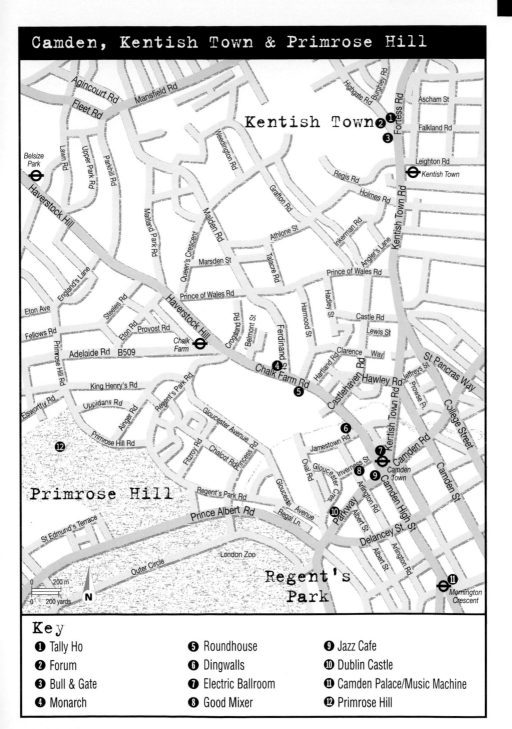

Key

1. Tally Ho
2. Forum
3. Bull & Gate
4. Monarch
5. Roundhouse
6. Dingwalls
7. Electric Ballroom
8. Good Mixer
9. Jazz Cafe
10. Dublin Castle
11. Camden Palace/Music Machine
12. Primrose Hill

Above: The Music Machine is now known as the Camden Palace.

together here as Strontium 90. The next month they renamed themselves the Police.

In the mid-1990s, Camden's Parkway became the epicentre of all things Britpop. Both Blur and Oasis used to drink nearby at the **Good Mixer** pub, 30 Inverness Street. Madness were regular performers at the **Dublin Castle**, 94 Parkway, when they started out. This local old Victorian pub still hosts bands every night and, according to one performer, has 'a vague feeling that it was often a happening place once'. The night that Blur played here, in May 1995, is fully documented in a framed newspaper story behind the bar. The **Jazz Cafe**, at 5 Parkway, opened in December 1990 and quickly established itself as a top jazz, soul and R&B venue. **Dingwalls** in Camden Lock has been a popular club and venue for many years. It was a pub-rock stronghold and in 1983 REM played their UK debut here.

KENTISH TOWN

It may be dwarfed by the mighty **Forum** (formerly the Town and Country Club) virtually next door but the **Bull & Gate** at 389 Kentish Town Road is a respected venue that boasts three bands nightly and prides itself on breaking new acts. Nirvana and Suede, named after an old dry-cleaners shop in Stoke Newington, played early gigs here. Most of the indie acts that play here are entirely unknown so you can usually find somewhere to sit, but one never knows, they could be playing at the Forum in just a few years time. The music room is basic but it does at least have chairs along each side in case the bands become too much to bear.

Regular gigsters say it's a good venue to play and the promoters have worked hard, even if they have to stuff three bands on a night to make ends meet. This was also an early venue for the Manic Street Preachers where they appeared in the same – or similar – boiler suit chic that featured on their debut record sleeve.

Right: The Town and Country Club, now the Forum, continues to attract the big names.

Below: Oscar Brown at the Jazz Cafe, now one of London's top jazz, soul and R&B venues.

> The only time I took acid voluntarily was at the UFO, it was jolly nice. I've always rather flippantly said since that it was rather like going to Stratford-on-Avon; once you'd done it, you didn't need to do it again.

JOHN PEEL

The venue was only a third full that night, and from a musician's point of view these sorely under-attended gigs are still a problem. One jobbing musician wonders whether these small crowds are to do with the rise of dance culture and the fact that it doesn't occur to Londoners to go to a pub venue just to catch some live music. 'If you have an audience at all then it's one that you have brought yourself,' he says. 'I have honestly seen bands, probably from out of town and unaware of the system, playing to empty rooms. There seem to be more and more venues, and the venues try to cram three or four bands on a night in an attempt to maximize the crowd brought by each band, but perhaps this serves only to remove the idea from Londoners' minds that there is anything special about live music.'

London's pub venues previously hosted jazz, folk and country and western gigs. Pub rock blasted on the scene and the likes of the Hope & Anchor, the Kensington, the Cock Tavern and the Lord Nelson became the breeding grounds for a motley assortment of jobbing musicians. The first pub rock venue was Kentish Town's **Tally Ho**, at 9 Fortess Road, an Irish pub where an American band called Eggs Over Easy got the pub rock ball rolling back in 1971. They originally came over from New York to make a record with Chas Chandler, former Animals' bassist and ex-Jimi Hendrix manager. Following contractual difficulties the band grew tired of studio-bound work and walked into this pub near their house in Kentish Town to secure a Monday night residency. This grew to four nights a week by the end of 1971. Early pub-rockers Brinsley Schwarz (featuring musician and producer Nick Lowe) began to play here as well. Lowe once said the pub rock phenomenon was simply 'the regrouping of a bunch of middle-class ex-Mods who'd been through the hippy undergound scene and realized it wasn't their cup of tea'. Pub rock stalwarts Dr Feelgood also made their London debut at the Tally Ho.

CHALK FARM

A poor man's Royal Albert Hall perhaps, the **Roundhouse**, at 100 Chalk Farm Road, was once a large storage warehouse for Gilby's gin. Built in 1847 by Robert Stephenson, this vast circular brick building started life as a railway engine turning shed. The Roundhouse opened as a concert venue on a cold night in October 1966, hosting the launch party for the *International Times* (*IT*), an underground newspaper started by John 'Hoppy' Hopkins and Barry Miles, who ran the Indica alternative bookshop and gallery in Mason's Yard. At the party, which was fancy dress, Paul McCartney arrived dressed in full Arab garb and Marianne Faithfull turned up as a nun. Guests were greeted with sugar cubes which all assumed contained LSD. They didn't, although there was plenty more inside. It was a huge event and the headliners were Pink Floyd supported by Soft Machine. Guests rollicked naked in a 56-gallon jelly, cast in a bathtub. Ah, those were the days.

Over a Christmas season in the late Sixties, the Who, the Move and Pink Floyd played the first 10 p.m.-till-dawn gig at the Roundhouse. The audience was largely a psychedelic crowd from Notting Hill and Bayswater. The Roundhouse became the regular venue for the psychedelic UFO club (see Tottenham Court Road) after its original venue closed. With over 2,000 people dancing about in a giant round barn, these gigs were the earliest form of raves in everything but clothes, music and choice of pills. Even Apple Corps booked the Roundhouse for the Beatles' return concerts in December 1968 and January 1969 but these dates were later scrapped when the Fab Four disagreed about returning to live performance.

Below: Two of the albums recorded by The Stranglers at The Roundhouse.

Many legends have made their debut here. The New Yardbirds played under their new name Led Zeppelin, in November 1968, headed by Robert Plant thrashing around his mane of golden hair. In February 1970, David Bowie performed solo for the first time with Tony Visconti, Mick Ronson and John Cambridge in his band. Elton John and his band played here in April 1970 at the Pop Proms when he supported Marc Bolan and T Rex. In July that year, *Oh! Calcutta!*, Kenneth Tynan's controversial nude revue containing a sketch written by John Lennon, opened at the Roundhouse. Lennon couldn't attend so he sent George Harrison's wife, model Pattie

Above: The Stones' *Between the Buttons* was shot on Primrose Hill at 5 a.m.

Boyd, on his behalf. Eric Clapton was there and it was for the first time that he met Pattie. Few people are lucky enough to have pop songs written about them but Pattie Boyd has notched up two – Eric Clapton's 'Layla' and George Harrison's 'Something'. Nearby, Madness posed in front of Chalk Farm Underground station for their album *Absolutely*.

The **Monarch,** at 49 Chalk Farm Road, is one of the best of London's current crop of pub venues. It is currently home to the promoters Barfly, probably the hottest source of happening new talent. There's live music upstairs every night, often featuring new and up-and-coming bands. Some well-known groups who started out here in recent years include Space and Kula Shaker.

> He was a very odd chap and certainly the standout one in the early days. He had this extraordinary hair on a big head, small neck, wide shoulders, no hips, Rupert the Bear trousers, rollneck sweaters – a look that was quite unique. He was capable of fantastic charm, then his dark side would emerge. He was the first to experiment with acid and it was beginning to have an effect.

GERED MANKOWITZ, PHOTOGRAPHER, ON BRIAN JONES

PRIMROSE HILL

Ah, nice… **Primrose Hill**, an ancient megalithic mound and one of London's most pleasant green spaces, and on a clear day you can see forever… Well, at least as far as the North Downs. One icy morning in November 1966, the Rolling Stones were photographed here for the cover on their *Between the Buttons* album. Never mind the horizon, it looks as though the Stones could barely see a few feet ahead of them. The picture is fuzzy round the edges, which probably reflected the band's craggy state at the time. Photographer Gered Mankowitz shot the pictures at 5.30 a.m. after the band had been working all-night at a recording session at Olympic Studios in Barnes. He distorted the photographic image using a home-made filter constructed of black card, glass and vaseline, so that the Stones appeared to dissolve into the landscape. 'Brian was lurking in his collar,' Mankowitz said years later. 'I was frustrated because it felt like we were on the verge of something really special, and he was messing it up. But the way that Brian appeared not to give a shit is exactly what the band was about.' *Between the Buttons* marked a high point in Mankowitz's relationship with the Stones. Local boys Madness were also photographed on Primrose Hill for the cover of their 1982 album *Rise and Fall.* They looked their usual wacky selves and certainly more with it than the Stones.

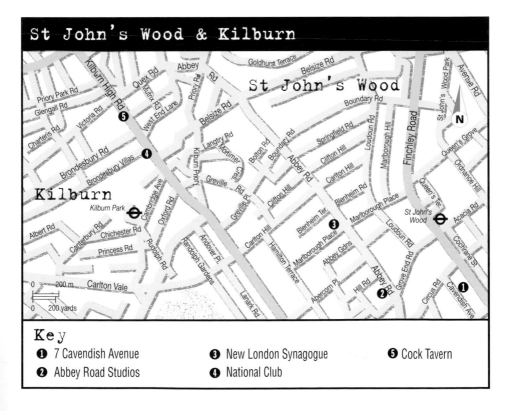

St John's Wood & Kilburn

Key

❶ 7 Cavendish Avenue   ❸ New London Synagogue   ❺ Cock Tavern
❷ Abbey Road Studios   ❹ National Club

ST JOHN'S WOOD

Cavendish Avenue, St John's Wood: all original features, all mod cons, only a few minutes away from Lords Cricket Ground, five minutes from Abbey Road Recording Studios, first viewer will take… Paul McCartney thought so in 1965. While John, George and Ringo left the bustle of London and moved to the country, McCartney stayed and set up home in an officially listed building at **7 Cavendish Avenue**, which he bought for £40,000. In August, he moved in with his girlfriend at the time, Jane Asher. He still owns the house, although he has not lived there since moving out to the country with his family in the late 1970s. McCartney wrote several songs here including 'Sergeant Pepper', 'Helter Skelter' and 'Penny Lane'. One summer night Paul gave an impromptu performance of 'Blackbird' to fans waiting outside. A thrilled audience heard Paul singing and playing an acoustic guitar from the open window of the top floor music room. It was here that many Lennon and McCartney compositions started life.

ABBEY ROAD

Who would have thought a simple zebra crossing in a leafy part of North London would become London's most famous rock'n'roll landmark and such a cultural icon? Just as every Muslim is encouraged to make a pilgrimage to the Hajj once in their lifetime, every Beatles' fan the world

Below: Officially still the EMI Studios, but now known universally as Abbey Road Studios simply because everyone calls them that.

Above: Around the world Abbey Road has become synonymous with The Beatles. Fans leave their personal tributes on every available space of the north-west London road sign.

over would like to visit the hallowed ground of Abbey Road and London NW8. All year, the EMI Studios (**Abbey Road Studios**) at 3 Abbey Road are barely visible behind spraypaint and affectionate graffiti. The reason is simple: The Beatles recorded virtually all of their songs here in Studio Two. It started on 11 September 1962, when the Fabs recorded 'Love Me Do' at the studios. The following year they recorded their debut album *Please Please Me* at the studios in just 13 hours.

Pink Floyd, Sting and Paul Weller have recorded here, and Liam and Noel Gallagher of Oasis (some might say a Beatles tribute band) are both self-confessed fans of the Fab Four. They even moved to live in the area because of their heroes. It was at the Abbey Road junction with Grove End Road that the four Beatles were photographed on a zebra crossing during a break from recording the *Abbey Road* album. The cover photograph was the result of a ten-minute shoot by freelance photographer Iain Macmillan, a friend of John and Yoko's. On the morning of 8 August 1969, Macmillan balanced himself and his Hasselblad camera up a stepladder in the middle of Abbey Road. He only had a few attempts to get it right. Macmillan took six shots of the Beatles walking back and forth across the zebra but only one emerged in which they did not appear out of step. This image became the front cover of the group's last recorded album, released on 26 September 1969. The original plan was to call it *Everest* after a brand of menthol cigarettes smoked by the engineer, Geoff Emerick, and fly the Fab Four out to the Himalayas for a cover shot. However, this idea was abandoned as calling it *Abbey Road* was a cheaper and easier alternative.

Some Beatles aficionados claim the Fab Four were making a deliberate statement on the cover and wished to be seen walking away from the studios. The pedestrian crossing on which they made their feelings known is the most famous in the world and every day since 1969 it has attracted Beatles' fans from just about everywhere. Some even imitate Paul McCartney and take their shoes off. You must do your own thing, but emulating Macca and removing one's footwear is only really advisable in the summer months, if at all. Seriously though, if your heart is set on pictures it's worth noting that Abbey Road is increasingly busy and there have been several accidents caused by fans not looking out for traffic. Imitation is, of course, the sincerest form of flattery but not a wise move unless you want to risk the full wrath and pent-up aggression of London's disgruntled motorists. Your best bet is to do it very early one Sunday morning in the summer. And don't bother asking Abbey Road for a tour of the building. They remain busy commercial studios so, although they totally understand the interest, staff are unable to help out. Why should they? Would you like total strangers poking around your place of work? They do not discourage people from taking photographs of the building from the pavement. However, if the studios are busy those who insist on having their photo taken on the steps might be moved on. The outside wall of Abbey Road Studios has a history all of its own. Management accept graffiti and messages from fans all over the world. In winter, the walls are normally repainted every three months, but during the summer it can be as often as every fortnight. A photograph is taken before every respray – so expect a book on Abbey Road graffiti one day.

It is impossible to measure the importance of the Beatles to Abbey Road Studios, or indeed vice versa. The Studios never officially changed their name from plain and simple EMI Studios but during the 1970s people started calling it Abbey Road Studios so they adopted the name.

The album opens with 'Come Together', billed as a Lennon–McCartney composition although it was actually written entirely by John. But Morris Levy, head of music publishers Big Seven Music Corporation, disagreed. Levy said the lyrics of the song were suspiciously close to Chuck Berry's 1956 song, 'You Can't Catch Me'. Lennon admitted being influenced by Berry while writing 'Come Together', but denied plagiarizing his work. Nevertheless, Levy filed a suit against Lennon for copyright infringement and was victorious.

Abbey Road's other musical milestones include Pink Floyd's ground-breaking debut album, *Piper at the Gates of Dawn* (recorded at the same time as the Beatles did *Sgt Pepper's Lonely Hearts Club Band*) and their 1973 breakthrough album *Dark Side of the Moon*, still one of the best-selling albums ever. The short excerpts of dialogue throughout the album were the result of a questionnaire undertaken by Roger Waters, who recorded the answers and mixed the best into the album. One of the most memorable voices is the late Jerry Driscoll's lyrical Irish accent on 'The Great Gig in the Sky'. A popular porter at Abbey Road during the time of recording between June 1972 and January 1973, he claims, on the album, not to be worried by the prospect of dying. In more recent years, Abbey Road has hosted bands such as Travis and Radiohead (their *Kid A* album was mastered here) and remains one of London's top film-scoring facilities. It was the crew here who were behind soundtracks to the blockbusters *Chicken Run*, *Braveheart* and *Notting Hill*.

A little walk down the road (bare feet in the mode of Paul McCartney not recommended) is the **New London Synagogue** (33 Abbey Road). It was here, on 17 October 1967, that Brian Epstein's memorial service was held, attended by all four Beatles. Epstein had died a few days earlier in his Chelsea flat after a drugs overdose.

KILBURN

Long before it became known as the **National Club**, Kilburn's Gaumont State Theatre, at 195–199 Kilburn High Road, was the largest picture house in Europe when it opened in the 1930s. And with massive chandeliers it was certainly one of the most palatial. Its large stage also made it ideal for pop and rock concerts. Buddy Holly and Bill Haley and his Comets played here in the late 1950s, the Beatles in October 1964, and the Rolling Stones in November 1963.

The **Cock Tavern**, down the way at 125 Kilburn High Road was a regular venue for pub rockers Brinsley Schwarz, Ducks Deluxe and Ian Dury's locally-inspired Kilburn and the High Roads. The Mean Fiddler, 28a High Street, in nearby Harlesden, remains a popular venue today. The late Roy Orbison – the Big 'O' – played his last UK gig here in 1988.

Above: Pink Floyd's *Piper at the Gates of Dawn* was another famous album recorded at EMI's Abbey Road studios.

WEST HAMPSTEAD

It's been the site of rehearsal studios for ENO (that's the English National Opera, not Brian Eno) since 1980, but the former **Decca Studios** at 165 Broadhurst Gardens were best-known as the location of the Beatles' notorious failed audition on New Year's Day 1962. For many years, this building was the main recording studio for Decca Records, who declined the Fabs because they had space to take on only one group. Instead they decided on Brian Poole and the Tremeloes, whose sound they believed was more marketable. Guitar groups were on the way out reckoned Decca. Later the tapes of the Beatles' audition led to a deal with EMI and Decca artist and repertoire executive Dick Rowe became known as 'the man who turned down the Beatles'. His reputation was saved a year later when he signed a new group called the Rolling Stones, ironically on George Harrison's recommendation. John Mayall's Bluesbreakers, featuring Eric Clapton, recorded here, with Eric reading *The Beano* on the cover. In September 1964, the

> It was not the posh end of Hampstead, but those awful Victorian dwellings around the back of the station. There was no running water and really desperate people lived up there. It was awful. I liked it. It was better than home.

JOHNNY ROTTEN, DESCRIBING
HIS HAMPSTEAD SQUAT

19-year-old Rod Stewart went to Decca's studios to make his solo recording debut. David Bowie auditioned here in September 1966, recording some of his early songs.

Cream's London debut in the summer of 1966 took place at a rhythm and blues club called **Klooks Kleek**, above a pub called the Railway Hotel at 100 West End Lane. The venue had a problem booking some of the big name bands like the Yardbirds, because it was strictly a licensed pub club and the Yardbirds attracted an audience too young to be admitted. In the 1970s it became the Moonlight Club, a punk and new wave venue. The Stone Roses made their debut here in October 1984 supporting Pete Townshend.

HAMPSTEAD

In 1975, Sex Pistol frontman Johnny Rotten lived in a squat with his friend Sid Vicious, at **42a Hampstead High Street**, where he started to pen some lyrics: 'It was not the posh end of Hampstead, but those awful Victorian dwellings around the back of the station,' recalled Rotten. 'There was no running water and really desperate people lived up there. It was awful. I liked it. It was better than home.'

After their first American tour in June 1964, both Mick Jagger and Keith Richards moved to Hampstead and shared the ground floor flat at **10a Holly Hill**. They stayed there until the spring of 1965. Three years later the scene of lavish debauchery that adorned the cover of the Rolling Stones' 1968 album, *Beggars Banquet* – Brian Jones' last – was shot inside the interior at Sarum Chase on Hampstead Heath. Photographer Michael Joseph shot in colour but Mick Jagger preferred the black-and-white pictures. The building was owned by the Church Commission, who demanded assurances before the shoot that there would be no naked women involved. No nudes, sure, but it's unlikely the clerics got down and bopped to the album's opener track, 'Sympathy for the Devil'.

There's a part of Hampstead that could easily be renamed Mansions-R-Us. First, there's Foley House, at **11 East Heath Road**, home of Pink Floyd drummer Nick Mason. Boy George moved to the Gothic house at **17 Well Road** after making shed-loads of money with Culture Club and in his solo career. It was also here that George was arrested during his heroin addiction. Sting's old home in the 1980s was at 108 Frognal, before he moved to Highgate. Within easy walking distance of Hampstead Heath is an exclusive road, off Frognal, called Oakhill Park.

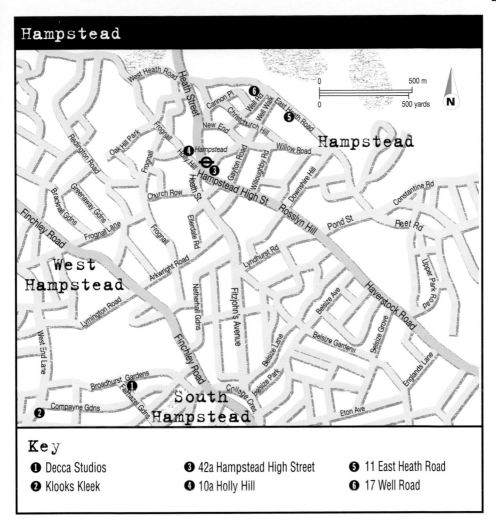

Hampstead

Key

❶ Decca Studios
❷ Klooks Kleek
❸ 42a Hampstead High Street
❹ 10a Holly Hill
❺ 11 East Heath Road
❻ 17 Well Road

George Michael lived here in the 1990s in a house that drops down the hill from the road allowing some privacy. Beatles' producer George Martin converted an old church in the early 1990s for his new Air Studios. Visitors have included Elton John and Dire Straits.

MILL HILL

Future rock stars take note – if you want to guarantee a decent shrine that celebrates your full genius and is situated in a decent location, make sure you have it erected while you're still around. As rock graves go it might not be on a par with the Pere Lachaise cemetery in Paris where Jim Morrison is buried, but there's a loving tribute to 1950s icon Billy Fury in Mill Hill cemetery. Fans who consider the Liverpool-born Fury to be Britain's greatest rocker have done their utmost to keep his grave tidy while much of its surroundings have become a mass of weeds. The cemetery was one of those infamously sold by Westminster council's Lady Porter in the late 1980s for one penny to a construction company. An ombudsman eventually forced the council to buy them back – at the going commercial rate.

WILLESDEN

Rod Stewart cut his first album, *An Old Raincoat Will Never Let You Down*, at what was then Morgan Studios, 169–171 Willesden High Road. Lou Reed recorded here, as did Blind Faith (featuring Eric Clapton on guitar), who held their first rehearsal and recording sessions here in February 1969. Paul McCartney turned up to record parts of his first solo album, the imaginatively-titled *McCartney* in spring 1970, soon followed by Ringo Starr, whose debut *Sentimental Journey* was partly completed at the studios. The Kinks played sessions for *Lola Vs Powerman And the Money Go Round Part One* here in 1970. They intended their recording to be for demos only, but the sessions ended up on the album.

WEMBLEY

For many, the twin towers of Wembley Stadium conjure up great memories of Britain's finest sporting moment, the 1966 World Cup Final, when Sir Geoff Hurst put three past the Germans. English football fans have gone on about this event ever since, in the absence of winning any recent international silverwear. There was also a memorable afternoon

in the 1970s when daredevil motorcyclist Evel Knievel crashed after his attempt to leap over umpteen red London buses failed. But Wembley scored its best goal on 13 July 1985, as millions of people around the world helped contribute to famine relief in the developing world during the extraordinary Live Aid concert organized by Sir Bob Geldof, former Boomtown Rats' frontman. More than 1.4 billion people across 170 countries watched it on television, raising millions for the starving in Ethiopia. It was a Woodstock concert for the post-hippy generation, when people could actually change the world. Geldof was officially sanctioned a saint a year later when he was given an honorary knighthood.

Opposite: Sir Bob Geldof became known around the world for organizing one of the biggest concerts ever.

Following their performance at Live Aid, Queen were judged the best band of the day. The world agreed that Freddie Mercury stole the show. Queen, who until then had failed to crack America, went stratospheric. But Wembley Stadium has always netted the big cats. From the 1971 Rock'n'Roll Festival featuring Little Richard, which attracted 50,000 fans, right up to more recent gigs by the Rolling Stones, Bruce Springsteen, Madonna and Michael Jackson, Wembley still packs 'em in. The stadium is an accountant's Utopia: one gig here saves doing an awful lot of nights at smaller venues. You can kill 100,000 birds with one stone, so to speak.

Next to the sporting goliath, Wembley's Empire Pool (Empire Way), now the Wembley Arena, has been a leading London concert venue since the 1950s. 'The Day Pop Came Back' screamed the headlines in the wake of T Rex's two concerts held here on 18 March 1972. TRextasy was never quite so ecstatic again. The Beatles played their last UK gig here at the *NME* Poll Winners' concert in May 1966. The high point of a Styx concert here in the 1980s was AC/DC's album *Back in Black* played during the interval.

Wembley's most famous musical son and certainly its most outrageous was the late Keith Moon who grew up at 134 Chaplin Road and went to Alperton Secondary School.

HARROW

The Who's destructive onstage routines, smashing up their equipment, became an integral part of their live performances. They honed the act at the former Railway Hotel pub by Harrow and Wealdstone tube station. Since the 1950s, the Railway hosted a series of jazz clubs, but in 1962 it started a rhythm and blues club called the Bluesday Club. It was at a gig here that the mop-fringed Pete Townshend smashed his guitar into the ceiling for the first time. As it got a good reaction from the audience the group decided to incorporate it into their act.

Former students of Harrow College of Art on the High Street have included Rolling Stones' drummer Charlie Watts, who studied graphic design in 1961. Sex Pistols' manager, Malcolm McLaren, attended in 1963. It was here that he met Vivienne Westwood and they became partners, later establishing a boutique on the King's Road where the Sex Pistols were formed.

The Beatles met Cliff Richard for the first time in April 1963, at the former home of Bruce Welch, rhythm guitarist in the Shadows, at 157 Headstone Lane in North Harrow. The Fabs were invited to Welch's party to celebrate the end of the Shadows' successful UK tour.

PINNER

Rock superstar Elton John started out life as a pudgy-faced only child called Reginald Dwight, living in Pinner, an ultra-conservative surburb 12 miles north-west of central London. For his first five years he lived with his mother Sheila Dwight at 55 Pinner Hill Road, a two-storey, semi-detached council house. Young Reg was enrolled in Reddiford, a private school. He later attended Pinner County Grammar School (now Heathfield Girls School). The school housed a Steinway grand piano and Reg's music teacher soon recommended him for a scholarship for weekend tutoring in the Royal Academy of Music's junior programme.

In 1962, Elton moved with his mother and her partner, a decorator and handyman called Fred Farebrother, into a ground floor flat at 30 Frome Court, Pinner Road. Much later, Elton John moved back here with songwriting partner Bernie Taupin for nearly two years after they left Islington. They wrote many of their early numbers here, including 'Your Song'. Two years later a teenage Elton started playing professionally, securing himself regular weekend gigs as a pub pianist at the Northwood Hills Hotel, a mock Tudor building about three times the size of a standard pub with a circular driveway. It was here he first learned to win crowds over, playing Chuck Berry and Jerry Lee Lewis numbers.

Below: A 27-year-old Elton John taking on the role of Pinner's piano man.

NORTH &
NORTH-EAST

Ever wondered how Rod Stewart pioneered his wild hairstyle or where the Small Faces sung about in 'Itchycoo Park'? This is not such a musical backwater as you may think. There is the Muswell Hill of the Kinks, Rod Stewart and folk-rockers Fairport Convention and London's most treasured pub venue, Islington's Hope & Anchor, and the Camden Head. And who could forget the late lamented Rainbow Theatre in Finsbury Park or good old Alexandra Palace? And of all places, it was an old club in Forest Gate where Jimi Hendrix penned his classic 'Purple Haze'.

Rod Stewart's trademark hairstyle, tight pants and gravelly voice put him in a class of his own.

ISLINGTON

Elton John's 'Someone Saved My Life Tonight' was inspired by the period during 1968 in which the musician lived in the basement flat at **29 Furlong Road** with songwriter Bernie Taupin. The song was believed to be about Elton's suicide attempt at the flat, when he tried to gas himself by sticking his head in an oven. He was depressed, stressed and feeling trapped at the thought of marriage to his girlfriend Linda Woodrow, heiress to the Epicure pickle empire. Later Elton revealed the song was an ode to bluesman Long John Baldry, who spotted Elton John's homosexuality early on. Baldry told Elton that if he went through with the marriage he would ruin not one but two lives.

Another landmark of British punk was Pathway Studios, at 2a Grosvenor Avenue. This small eight-track recording studio opened in 1970 and is still there today, pretty much unchanged from the time when the likes of Siouxsie and the Banshees turned up to record the classic 'Hong Kong Garden'. Nick Lowe produced fellow Stiff Records performer Elvis Costello's debut album *My Aim Is True* here. Costello recorded the album during his holidays and sick days taken from his computer job at the Elizabeth Arden factory in Acton. The demo tape for Dire Straits' 'Sultans of Swing' was recorded at Pathway and after the tapes were aired on BBC Radio London the band were offered a recording contract with Phonogram.

Below: The Camden Head pub was an early rehearsal venue for the Kinks.

They didn't need no education. Twenty-three pupils from the fourth form at Islington Green School missed out on it for one day when they sang with Pink Floyd's David Gilmour on 'Another Brick in The Wall (Part Two)' for the album *The Wall*. Pink Floyd recorded their dulcet tones at **Britannia Row Studios**, a converted chapel at 35 Britannia Row. The voice of the teacher on the track was a real teacher from the school. Joy Division's 1980 album *Closer* was recorded here and the studios have also been used by Tori Amos and Motorhead.

In the early 1960s, the Kinks used to rehearse at the **Camden Head** pub, 2 Camden Walk, an old Victorian hostelry that nestles amongst the antique dealers of Camden Passage. Their drummer Mick Avory was first auditioned after responding to an advert in *Melody Maker*. 'Drummer wanted for smart go-ahead group'. In late October 1963, they finally persuaded Beatles' manager Brian Epstein to watch them perform. 'As we went through our tiny repertoire of blues and cover songs, Epstein looked at us all individually like a man trying to spot a quality racehorse at an auction,' recalled Kinks' guitarist Dave Davies.

Islington's **Screen on the Green** is an esteemed art-house cinema at 83 Upper Street, but at the end of August 1976, it was the site of a punk explosion, the venue of the first public performance of the Clash at a mid night-till-dawn spectacular. Wearing slogans and splattered with paint, the Clash appeared alongside the Sex Pistols, Siouxsie and the Banshees and the Buzzcocks.

One of London's best known pub venues, Islington's **Hope & Anchor** (207 Upper Street) became a leading venue of punk rock in the late 1970s. Locals will tell you that barring Richard Clayderman and the James Last Orchestra, just about anyone who was anyone played here. The Clash, the Damned, the Stranglers, and the Sex Pistols were here twice. The Hope & Anchor was previously a seminal pub rock venue that saw the best-known acts play simple rhythm and blues. Spirited

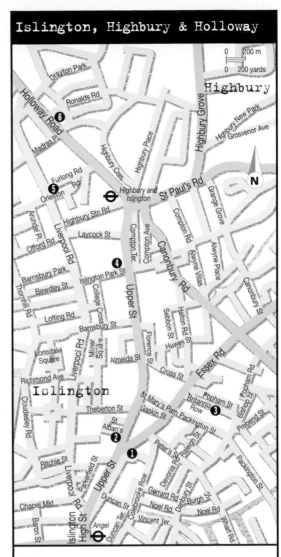

Islington, Highbury & Holloway

Highbury

Key
1. Camden Head
2. Screen on the Green
3. Britannia Row Studios
4. Hope & Anchor
5. 29 Furlong Road
6. Lord Nelson

Above: Top pub-rockers Dr Feelgood had a no. 1 album with *Stupidity* in 1976.

Seventies acts such as Dr Feelgood from Canvey Island summed up pub rock with their frontman, the late Lee Brilleaux and manic Wilko Johnson with his trademark staccato guitar work.

When it came to recording, many pub rock groups discovered it was difficult to capture the excitement of sweaty live gigs. *Live at the Hope & Anchor* albums were released, capturing the rough and ready quality of the bands and the crowds who came along to cheer them. With the exception of Ace's 1974 hit 'How Long', none of the pub rockers had a major hit until Dr Feelgood's live album, *Stupidity*, topped the charts in October 1976. Dave Robinson, co-founder of Stiff Records with Jake Riviera, built an eight-track studio above the venue. In the summer of 1975, Graham Parker and the Rumour started recording. In later years, Joy Division played an early London date in December 1978 and the following year Dexy's Midnight Runners and U2 played their first London gigs here, with no more than nine people in the audience. It was also an early venue for Dire Straits.

The local Environmental Health Authority eventually closed the music room down. It reopened in 1996, when the council granted another music licence, and once again you can watch indie and rock bands play here until midnight, six nights a week. One regular performer remarked on how the Hope & Anchor's stage is smaller than ever these days. 'We're a five-piece and we can only fit on the stage if we stand sideways!' But as for the venue, he says, it is just resting on its laurels. A plaque on the wall proudly announces that Ian Dury's first band, the pioneering pub rockers, Kilburn and the High Roads, once played at the establishment. Sadly they call him Ian 'Drury'. 'This tells you all you need to know,' says our performer.

> ❝ We're a five-piece and we can only fit on the stage if we stand sideways! ❞
>
> HOPE AND ANCHOR REGULAR

HIGHBURY

A small studio in the former Rank Charm School was, ironically, the studios in 1977 where the Sex Pistols recorded their only album *Never Mind the Bollocks*, with legendary producer Chris Thomas. Wessex Sound Studios, at 106 Highbury New Park, was a recording studio since the late 1960s. Ringo Starr came here in November 1969 to tape parts of his solo album *Sentimental Journey* and George Harrison also recorded solo material. The Clash recorded *London Calling* here in 1979.

HOLLOWAY

A strange death visited this part of North London in early February 1967, when 36-year-old Joe Meek, composer and pop group promoter in the early to mid-1960s, was found shot dead in his RGM Recording Studios above 304 Holloway Road. Meek was a production genius who created space age, sonic pop with hits like 'Telstar', recorded by his group, The Tornados, which is the best-selling instrumental of all time and the first single by a British group to top the American charts, and 'Johnny Remember Me', which was a tribute to Buddy Holly. It turned out that he had shot his landlady and then turned the gun on himself, exactly eight years after Holly's death.

The **Lord Nelson** pub at 100 Holloway Road was another important 1970s regular pub rock venue. Names that featured regularly included the likes of Ian Dury's Kilburn and the High Roads, Ducks Deluxe and Dr Feelgood.

Above: Everyone barring the James Last Orchestra appears to have played Islington's Hope & Anchor.

FINSBURY PARK

Plenty of rock acts have trodden the boards of the **Rainbow Theatre** (232 Seven Sisters Road) over the years. One of London's premier rock venues, even some of the biggest names were happy to play this 3,000-capacity venue. The Rainbow resounded to the screams of teenage fans of the Beatles, David Bowie and the Osmonds. Now it belongs to the Universal Church of the Kingdom of God, a global evangelical church which originated in Brazil in the 1970s; gospel tunes now offer protection from black magic and witchcraft – quite a contrast from a Dire Straits concert.

The dressing rooms never had flow diagrams pinned to the wall demonstrating how to play guitar with your teeth and the management didn't supply lighter fuel, but the Rainbow is probably most famous as the venue, in March 1967, where Jimi Hendrix first burnt his Fender Stratocaster guitar on stage as he played 'Wild Thing'. He received slight burns, but it was well worth it. The audience loved it and the resulting exposure made it part of his act. Maybe Hendrix's motives were rather more basic than artistic and he was just trying to warm himself up, because the Rainbow had a reputation for being draughty.

After refurbishment in 1971, the Rainbow was launched in the same building as the old Finsbury Park **Astoria**, which doubled as a cinema and concert venue. The Byrds played

Left: Get those heads banging! No, not Jimi Hendrix but Phil Lynott and Thin Lizzy at the Rainbow.

here in 1965, billed as America's answer to the Beatles and supported by Donovan, himself touted as Britain's equivalent to Bob Dylan. The Rainbow Theatre never just catered for popular music fans as proved when jazz drummer Art Blakey and his Jazz Messengers played in that same year. It has hosted many classic acts. The Beatles played here a total of 18 times and Pink Floyd performed *Dark Side of the Moon* to an unsuspecting audience in February 1972, a year before the album was released. Eric Clapton played his famous comeback concert in January 1973, organized by Pete Townshend. Since mid-1971 Clapton, crippled by heroin addiction, had become a virtual recluse at his home, Hurtwood Edge, near his birthplace in Ripley, Surrey. Although the concert was a great success it began ominously when Clapton turned up late and the audience feared he had bottled it. When he arrived, he blamed the delay on his increased weight, which had meant he couldn't get into his special stage trousers and they had had to be altered.

It was a hard act to follow, but ex-Small Faces drummer Kenney Jones made his live debut with the Who in May 1979 at the Rainbow, several months after the death of Keith Moon. The

Clash played an important gig here on the first night of their White Riot tour on 9 May 1977. Supported by the Jam, it was a watershed gig for the West London punk band who had previously only played much smaller clubs. The Damned played their farewell bash at the Rainbow in April 1978.

Another strange death visited these parts in May 1974 when the British rhythm and blues pioneer and Sixties organ king, Graham Bond, threw himself under a Piccadilly line train at **Finsbury Park tube station**. He was depressed, suffering from drug addiction and an obsession with the black arts convinced him that he was being chased by demons. In 1965, Bond claimed the organ had replaced the big band and though he achieved little commercial success with his Graham Bond Organisation, his influence was widespread amongst Sixties musicians from the Stones to Eric Clapton. Finsbury Park itself is the venue for the annual open-air Fleadh concert.

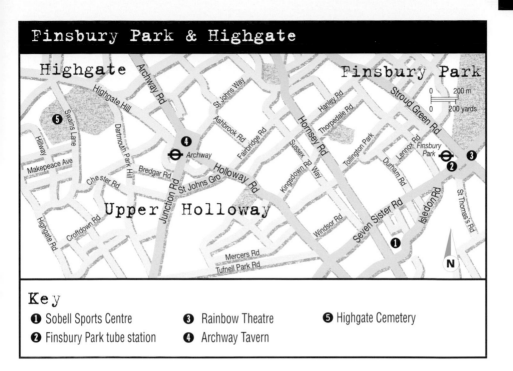

Finsbury Park & Highgate

Key

1. Sobell Sports Centre
2. Finsbury Park tube station
3. Rainbow Theatre
4. Archway Tavern
5. Highgate Cemetery

HIGHGATE

Highgate Cemetery in Swain's Lane is known the world over as the last resting place of Karl Marx. The cemetery does not loom large in musical circles, except for an early non-musical gig for the young Rod Stewart. Before he began singing professionally Rod the Mod had a summer job digging graves in the cemetery's eastern part. It was only for three weeks and it poured with rain most of the time, the singer later recalled. As part of an initiation ritual, his colleagues put him in a coffin and closed the lid. 'That really scared me but I've had no fear of death since. It cured me,' said Rod. 'I've always believed the only way to tackle that kind of fear is to face up to it.'

The last of five children, Rod Stewart was born in the family home at **507 Archway Road**, which is now demolished, on 10 January 1945. He lived above his parents' newsagents and proved terrible at selling newspapers. However, he got better at it, later on in life, when he became famous and sold newspapers in another sense. The draughty, near hurricane conditions that haunt the escalators at Highgate underground station may well have been responsible for Rod Stewart's distinctive devil-may-care hairstyle. Stewart used to catch the tube into town from Highgate station and when a train came in, it would blow his backcombed and lacquered hair all over the place. At this point, Rod would attempt to hold it in place with his hands.

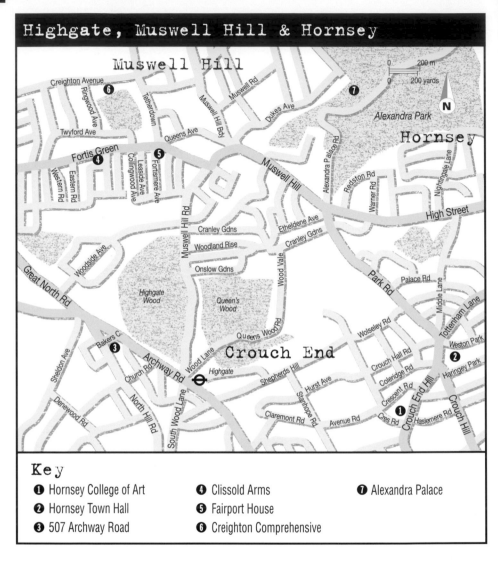

Highgate, Muswell Hill & Hornsey

Key

1. Hornsey College of Art
2. Hornsey Town Hall
3. 507 Archway Road
4. Clissold Arms
5. Fairport House
6. Creighton Comprehensive
7. Alexandra Palace

When the Jam headlined two CND benefits at the **Sobell Sports Centre** on Hornsey Road, in December 1981, the poor reaction of the crowd to the support acts the Questions and Bananarama helped hasten Paul Weller's decision to split up the band. Weller admitted he hated the 'we want the Jam!' mentality of the fans.

A number of the Kinks' songs penned by Ray Davies were inspired by his local North London surroundings. Even the cover shots for their 1971 album *The Muswell Hillbillies* were taken in the **Archway Tavern**, Archway Close, which is still there today.

MUSWELL HILL

Folk-rockers Fairport Convention coined their name after a house in Muswell Hill on the corner of Fortis Green Road and Fortismere Avenue. **Fairport House** belonged to the doctor father of Simon Nicol, the group's guitarist.

The more famous half of the Kinks, Dave and Ray Davies, grew up in a working class household in a run-down area of Muswell Hill at 6 Denmark Terrace, Fortis Green. Ray Davies was the first boy born to a family of six girls in 1944. Ray created the song, 'You Really Got Me' on the piano in

Above: After a gig in Highgate, Weller made up his mind to disband the Jam.

the living room. Their house was opposite the **Clissold Arms** at 115 Fortis Green, which is still there today. The young Ray and Dave performed regular instrumental duets for family and friends here and at their father's local. Ray played the lead parts as his younger brother bashed out the rhythm. They knocked out such tunes as 'Sweet Georgia Brown' and others later recorded as demos at Regent Sound on Denmark Street.

> And so I was out of school, liberated at 15, and savouring the street life and nightlife of London. Anything could happen in those carefree days. It was the dawn of 1963, the beginning of an era of rock'n'roll we could not have predicted. Teenage boys swarmed London looking for action and I was one of them.

DAVE DAVIES

Ray Davies went to William Grimshaw Grammar School (now **Creighton Comprehensive** in Creighton Avenue), and later described another former pupil of the school, Rod Stewart, as the Elvis Presley of Muswell Hill. Rod failed his 11-plus exams and went to the secondary modern near his home. His macho image was established early on: he played a lot of football and was later an apprentice for Brentford FC. Elected a form prefect, he later lost the position through the time-honoured schoolboy prank of letting off a fire extinguisher.

Dave Davies of the Kinks attended the same school and he faired even worse, expelled after being found in the long grass of Hampstead Heath with a young lady during school hours. Ray was in the year above Stewart, and he met Pete Quaife (later the Kinks' guitarist) while at the school. They were in the same music class and later formed his first band, the Ray Davies Quartet. Throughout his fame Ray Davies has continued to live in Muswell Hill, never electing to live the big-house-in-the-country lifestyle like so many other stars.

Opposite: A psychedelic experience for Jimi Hendrix is captured on this bill poster in all its glory.

Below: Ex-Hornsey pupil Stuart Goddard became better known as Adam Ant.

Rod Stewart stayed in Muswell Hill when he bought his first home in 1969. With the advance money for his solo albums, he bought a colonial-style house near his family in Ellington Road. When he joined the Faces in June 1969, the band used it as a rendezvous and were sometimes to be seen and heard strumming their guitars on the balcony. While living here he wrote a number of songs for the Faces, which included 'Stay With Me' and 'Maggie May'. Stewart has said this latter song was about losing his virginity as a 16-year-old to an older, rather large woman at the Beaulieu Jazz Festival. These tracks launched his solo career.

Now a recognized name, Stewart bought his parents a new house on Woodley Road, Muswell Hill and he moved into a four-bedroomed mock Tudor house in desirable Broad Walk, Winchmore Hill, with his first serious girl-friend, Dee Harrington. In 1972, when star-spotters discovered

his whereabouts and begun to make life in Broad Walk difficult, he moved to a 14-acre estate near Windsor Great Park, made up of 36 rooms and eight bathrooms. In 1975 he sold the estate and moved further afield to Hollywood with Britt Ekland.

HORNSEY

In 1972, Ray Davies purchased a run-down factory on the slopes of Alexandra Palace, at 84-86 Tottenham Lane, which became Konk Studios. It was here he developed the Kinks' concept albums of the 1970s: 'I suppose I wanted this studio to symbolize artistic freedom,' said Davies. 'Some kind of retaliation to the frustration I had encountered at art col-

Above: The Kinks' Ray Davies hailed from Muswell Hill – and has loyally remained there.

lege. The college itself was just up the road and it seemed appropriate that here was I, years later, after virtually being thrown out of that college, forming my own creative institution less than a mile away, on my terms with my money.' Konk Studios was to be the place where the Kinks could hang out together, play snooker, table-tennis, rehearse and record.

Ray Davies wrote 'You Really Got Me' at **Hornsey College of Art** (now part of MIddlesex Poly), 77 Crouch End Hill, in the early 1960s. After seeing bluesman Alexis Korner perform here, he formed his own blues group. Stuart Goddard (better known as Adam Ant) and Deep Purple bassist Roger Glover are both ex-pupils of the college.

In June 1971, with bassist John Deacon newly on board, Queen played their first gig at **Hornsey Town Hall**. The unlikely audience were the College of Estate Management.

ALEXANDRA PALACE

A huge gothic structure sandwiched between Muswell Hill and Wood Green, **Alexandra Palace** (or Ally Pally as it is affectionately known to most Londoners) was burnt to the ground just two weeks after it first opened in 1873. The original structure reopened two years later. Another fire nearly destroyed Ally Pally in July 1980, but it has been rebuilt in the same style. Part of the building was used by the BBC between the 1930s and the 1950s as a TV studio. Most famously, it was where the BBC's historic first broadcast took place in August 1936.

There were no broadcasts of Pink Floyd's two concerts at Alexandra Palace in July 1967, when former lead singer Syd Barrett's drug consumption publicly became a problem for the first time. At the second gig, fellow band members couldn't locate Syd. When he turned up, he managed to do a few numbers, freaked out onstage and was unable to continue performing properly. He was soon wheeled off. Barrett thought that his head was melting, a sensation brought on by a combination of hairwax and Mandrax tablets he'd concocted as a pomade which dissolved under the lights. It was reported he was suffering from nervous exhaustion.

The gigs were benefit concerts to fund the *International Times*' legal defence fund after the underground newspaper's offices had been raided by the police. 'Giant Benefit Against Fuzz Action' was the catchy ad in the *Melody Maker*. Despite being billed as an International Love-In Festival, the gigs were marred by violence. A few months earlier in April 1967, Pink Floyd had played a problem-free gig here at a psychedelic all-nighter called the 14-hour Technicolour Dream. The organizers made full use of Ally Pally's cathedral-like Great Hall, setting up a stage at each end with different attractions. An estimated 10,000-strong crowd moved around as new scenes developed. Over 40 bands were expected to play at the event. Some failed to appear, presumably too stoned to show up, although 20 bands showed including Pink Floyd, the Move and Arthur Brown. Once again, the concert had been staged to raise much-needed funds for the *International Times* in its battle against the unyielding establishment. The gig was a spiritual rather than financial success. Despite attracting the cream of the underground performers of the day to Ally Pally, most of the entrance money was pocketed by the ad hoc security and in the end almost nobody got paid.

STOKE NEWINGTON

Born Marc Feld, later Marc Bolan, the singer spent his childhood at 25 Stoke Newington Common until 1962. Bolan attended both Northwood Primary and William Wordsworth Secondary Modern schools.

HACKNEY

Marc Bolan claimed he carried Eddie Cochran's guitar at the Hackney Empire on Mare Street one Saturday morning in spring 1960. The American was in town to film an episode of *Oh Boy!* Tragically, Cochran died in a car crash a few weeks later.

Home-grown racism continued to be a problem throughout the 1970s, a time of heightened race awareness. Many years before Live Aid, Rock Against Racism sought to dispel racial tension, challenging prejudice and people who put forward racist ideas. On 30 April 1978, a political carnival and open-air concert was held in Hackney's Victoria Park, with sets by some of the biggest names of the day. The Clash, Steel Pulse, Sham 69, X-Ray Spex and Tom Robinson all played. The concert started with an assembly at Trafalgar Square followed by a six-mile march to Victoria Park. Organizers hoped for crowds of about 20,000 people to attend, but more like 100,000 people turned up. Another Rock Against Racism gig in September 1978 took place in Brockwell Park, featuring Aswad and Elvis Costello.

In 1973, John Lydon (later Johnny Rotten) went to Hackney College of Further Education. There he met John Beverley, the future Sex Pistol Sid Vicious, who was enrolled on a photography course.

FOREST GATE

It is widely believed that Jimi Hendrix wrote 'Purple Haze' in the dressing room of the Upper Cut, Forest Gate Centre, Woodgrange Road, a short-lived East London club run by boxer Billy Walker. A knockout opening week of gigs in December 1966 included the Who, Eric Burdon and the Animals and the Spencer Davis Group. The guitarist appeared on a bill poster as the 'Jimmy' Hendrix Experience. Some Hendrix fans claim the song, penned while waiting to go on stage for his Boxing Day gig and first played during that very show, does not refer to psychedelic drug experiences but to the lavender farms around Hendrix's native Seattle.

MANOR PARK

Steve Marriott, lead singer of the Small Faces, grew up at 26 Strone Road and was expelled from Sandringham Secondary Modern School for setting fire to the woodwork room, as you do. The nearby Manor Park was probably the inspiration for the band's classic 'Itchycoo Park'. The area was given the nickname, say some, because of its huge amount of stinging nettles. Others reckon it's a term East End kids gave to any local park where vagrants congregated. There has also been some speculation about the actual location of Itchycoo Park. Small Faces scholars identify it as Ilford Park, still at the bottom of Church Road but now minus the nettles. What is in no doubt, however, is that the 'dreaming spires' of the lyrics are not in East London. Fans say that guitarist Ronnie Lane saw them while staying in a hotel in Bristol or Oxford.

Steve Marriott landed a job at the J60 Music Bar, 445–57 High Street North, in 1965 and met both drummer Kenney Jones and songwriting partner Ronnie Lane, who were already in a band called the Outcasts. They needed a singer and with Marriott on board the Small Faces were formed. One afternoon in the shop, the three of them jammed under the guise of selling Ronnie Lane a bass guitar. Later, Marriott sold him an instrument at such a discounted price that he got the sack when his boss found out.

WALTHAMSTOW

In 1959, and with three 'O' levels under his belt, Ian Dury won a place at Walthamstow School of Art. Five years later, he progressed to the Royal College of Art, where his tutor was Peter Blake, who designed the album cover for *Sgt Pepper's Lonely Hearts Club Band*. After a stint teaching art in Canterbury, Dury formed his first band, Kilburn and the High Roads, in 1970. They played their last gig at Walthamstow Town Hall in June 1976, supported by the 101ers and the Stranglers.

Above: Lord Upminster, Ian Dury, was described as a Cockney Kurt Weill.

EDMONTON

Cream formed in July 1966 and played their first London gig at the Blue Opera Club, formerly the Cooks Ferry Inn on the River Lea Towpath, off Angel Road. Rod Stewart's manager Billy Gaff spotted Rod during a stint with Long John Baldry in the Hoochie Coochie Men. 'The first time I ever met Rod was in the dressing-room at the Cooks Ferry Inn, Edmonton. Rod had burned his face bright red from a sunlamp.' The Edmonton Regal saw gigs by the likes of Bill Haley, Jerry Lee Lewis and the Everly Brothers.

WEST

Remember Hyde Park's free concerts? Those were the wild and free days of the Rolling Stones and Pink Floyd... if you can remember them you probably weren't there. Welcome to the West London of garage bands from garageland who made some of punk's finest albums. It is home to the famous Notting Hill carnival, an old church hall where Pink Floyd first won their reputation and venues like the Hammersmith's Odeon and Palais. Take time to go way out west to the Ealing blues club where the Rolling Stones served their apprenticeship in a leaky basement.

West London was one of the original punk strongholds.

Everything from music to dress screamed rebellion.

EDGWARE ROAD

In the 1960s the Kinks went to desperate measures to impress Arthur Howes, the most influential concert promoter of the era, who booked tours for the Beatles. On New Year's Eve 1963, the Kinks, still called the Ravens, turned up at his favourite restaurant, the **Lotus House**, 61 Edgware Road, now the Al Dar Lebanese coffee shop, to play to him while he ate. Howes had a reputation for making instant decisions and fortunately he loved them. Suddenly the boys from Muswell Hill had a manager, a publishing deal and a booking agent.

BAYSWATER

When guitarist Richey Edwards of the Manic Street Preachers left London's **Embassy Hotel**, at 150 Bayswater Road (now the Jarvis London Embassy Hotel), on 1 February 1995, he and the hotel entered pop legend, as the star was never seen again. A Vauxhall Cavalier is an unusual choice of motor car for a rock star but, even so, his abandoned vehicle was found two weeks later at a motorway service station near the Severn Bridge. Like the Loch Ness Monster, there are 'sightings' of Edwards every few months, and the guitarist has been spotted in Goa, the Canary Islands and even Newport public library, just 15 miles from his hometown of Blackwood, Gwent. His disappearance followed a long period of depression in which Edwards famously inscribed the words '4 REAL' into his arm with a razor blade during an interview with *NME* journalist and BBC Radio 1 DJ Steve Lamacq.

George Harrison and John Lennon sampled LSD for the first time in 1965 at the home of Harrison's dentist at Flat 1, 2 Strathearn Place. They later went to the Ad Lib club off Leicester Square.

Little Venice may just be an excuse for estate agents to exercise their limited powers of description, but Pink Floyd guitarist David Gilmour has created his own palace by the canal on **Maida Avenue**, near Warwick Avenue. The current London home of the Pink Floyd frontman was originally two houses until he joined them together.

In 1977, **Stiff Records** was deemed the coolest record label on the planet. They operated out of their former offices at 32 Alexander Street, near Paddington

STIFF RECORDS

Recorded

Electrically

45 RPM
STEREO
'TURN IT UP'
Rock Music
Co Ltd/Street
Music Co
Made in England

BUY 6-A

℗ & © 1976
Stiff Records

Produced by
Nick Lowe at
Pathway for
Leather Nun
Productions

NEW ROSE (1.99)
(Brian James)
THE DAMNED

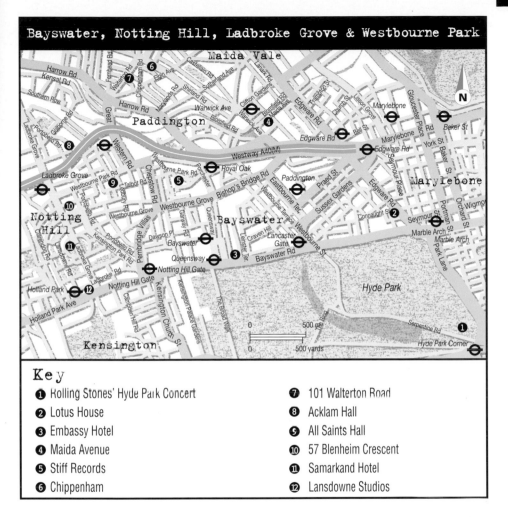

Bayswater, Notting Hill, Ladbroke Grove & Westbourne Park

Key

❶ Rolling Stones' Hyde Park Concert
❷ Lotus House
❸ Embassy Hotel
❹ Maida Avenue
❺ Stiff Records
❻ Chippenham

❼ 101 Walterton Road
❽ Acklam Hall
❾ All Saints Hall
❿ 57 Blenheim Crescent
⓫ Samarkand Hotel
⓬ Lansdowne Studios

Station. The offices of Blackhill Enterprises, who managed early Pink Floyd and staged free concerts in the 1960s, were also based here.

HYDE PARK

For each of the 250,000 people who attended the Rolling Stones' free concert in Hyde Park in early July 1969, there were thousands more who said they were there. Those who were really there still talk of this gig as one of the greatest events in British pop history. A memorable day and a milestone concert, not only for Mick Jagger's performance but also for the white dress he wore. Mick may have looked silly, but probably no more than the audience with their long hair and peace signs. Younger generations scoff nowadays, but everyone there captured the spirit of the age. The Stones played by the Serpentine Lake in the Park, just three days after their sacked guitarist (and founder) Brian Jones was found dead at the bottom of his swimming pool. The concert was dedicated to his memory and in a moment of poetry Jagger released thousands of butterflies into the afternoon sunshine. The Stones' new guitarist Mick Taylor had just joined the band and made his debut at this concert. Naïvely, perhaps, the Rolling Stones used the Hell's Angels to protect the stage at the gig. Six months later a similar decision to use them at the Altamont music festival in the USA had disastrous consequences when an Angel stabbed a reveller to death.

A year earlier, in June 1968, Pink Floyd gave London's then-largest free concert in the park to promote their album *A Saucerful of Secrets* and help revive their fortunes after Syd Barrett's departure from the band months earlier. Marc Bolan and T Rex also played the first of Blackhill Enterprises' free concerts on 29 June alongside Jethro Tull and Roy Harper. BBC disc jockey John Peel, at the time a resident DJ at the Middle Earth and good friend of Bolan, hired a boat and rowed on the Serpentine during the Floyd concert. 'And jolly nice it was too,' Peel recalled years later.

NOTTING HILL

Each year at the end of August, the streets around Notting Hill swell with the ranks of police officers and hundreds of thousands of party-goers as Europe's largest street party unfolds. Some embarrassed-looking policemen dance with revellers and mostly it's a peaceful if crowded event. The instigator was John Hopkins who, along with the *International Times* newspaper and more than a few immigrants from Trinidad, helped set up the first Notting Hill Carnival in 1966, when a pantomime horse was arrested by wary police. A decade later a dramatic incident at the end of the 1976 Notting Hill Carnival inspired 'White Riot', the first single by the Clash. On the last day of the carnival, singer Joe Strummer, bassist Paul Simonon and manager Bernie Rhodes were walking along when a conga-line of policemen came through the crowd. Someone threw a brick at the police

Opposite: Where did you get that dress? Not from the Hell's Angels, that's for sure. Mick Jagger centre stage at their famous free Hyde Park concert in the summer of 1969.

Above: The Clash's 'White Riot' urged whites to create a riot of their own.

and all hell broke loose. The crowd parted and the Clash were pushed onto wire netting. That summer had been very hot and there had been a lot of police pressure on the black community. Strummer's lyrics expressed his solidarity with the Rasta cause and envied the black urban population's ability to 'kick off'. He urged whites to fight back with a riot of their own, like the blacks had done at the carnival, otherwise they would get plastered over in society. The song established the Clash, in the public's mind, as authentic rebel rockers.

On 18 September 1970, the rock world was shocked by the news of the untimely death of Jimi Hendrix. The legendary guitarist took a fatal overdose in the flat of his girlfriend Monika Dannemann, at the **Samarkand Hotel**, 22 Lansdowne

Crescent. At around 7 a.m., Hendrix swallowed nine sleeping pills in the basement and later choked to death on his own vomit, while sleeping at the Cumberland Hotel (see Marble Arch).

Just two days after they signed to EMI in October 1976, the Sex Pistols went into **Lansdowne Studios** on Lansdowne Road to record their first single, 'Anarchy in the UK'. They were originally booked into Deep Purple's usual suite at Kingsway Studios, but that was cancelled when the Polydor deal fell though. EMI later tore up their contract too. Lansdowne had been a recording studio since the 1950s and it was here that the Faces recorded their first album, featuring Ronnie Wood and Rod Stewart.

A humble old church hall in Notting Hill had a huge influence on the career of Pink Floyd. From October 1966, the basement of **All Saints Hall** in Powis Gardens hosted London Free School's Light and Sound workshops, set up by John 'Hoppy' Hopkins. Then called the Pink Floyd Sound, they soon became the resident band and junked their cover versions in favour of Syd Barrett's original material. Here they developed their famous light show, with slide projections as an integral part of their live performance. The hall was never full, but it was always a wild scene, spacey and druggy. After the gigs the vicar swept up and shook the hands of punters as they left. Pink Floyd played regularly here and composed 'Interstellar Overdrive' and 'Stoned Alone'. When EMI scouts saw the group playing here they were offered a recording contract. Progressive rockers Hawkwind played their first concert at the All Saints Hall in August

Opposite bottom and below: The Notting Hill Carnival takes place each August and is Europe's biggest street party.

> This bunch of complete freaks walked in the door, out of their boxes and said, "Here, we're a band, can we play?"
>
> PROMOTER DOUG SMITH, ON HAWKWIND'S FIRST GIG

1969, under the name Group X. Hawkwind were attached to the Notting Hill area and named an album *Hall of The Mountain Grill* after a cafe on Portobello Road, a regular haunt for Bowie and Bolan. It was an impromptu jam to which they invited themselves: 'This bunch of complete freaks walked in the door, out of their boxes and said, "Here, we're a band, can we play?"' recalled promoter Doug Smith.

LADBROKE GROVE

Ladbroke Grove was a happening place in the late 1960s and naturally Marc Bolan wanted to be in the thick of it. In 1967, he moved into a flat at **57 Blenheim Crescent** with his wife June Child. It was here that he formed T Rex and wrote 'Ride A White Swan'. The flat was the scene of countless hippy happenings: a fairy on his mantelpiece, private conversations with an Eastern mystic and a Mushroom Studio.

WESTBOURNE PARK

Joe Strummer's pre-Clash band the 101ers didn't take their name from Room 101. Nothing so Orwellian. In the mid-1970s, he and the band lived and practised in a squat at **101 Walterton Road**. They played a lot of their early gigs in 1974 and 1975 in the **Chippenham** pub, 207 Shirland Road, a venue which is still very much in evidence today.

In September 1979, as one of west London's finest bands, the Clash, were recording their *London Calling* album, some strange noises could be heard emanating from the **Acklam Hall** in Westbourne Park. The venue played host to the world's first Bad Music Festival, two days of performances by such bands as the Blues Drango All-Stars, the Horrible Nurds and Living Dead No. 5 and assorted other nutters who were only in it for the bad publicity. Conspicuous by their absence were Peters and Lee, Go West, Kajagoogoo and a number of one-hit wonder bands.

KENSINGTON

Just off Kensington High Street, Rolling Stones' bassist Bill Wyman opened a restaurant at 1a Phillimore Gardens in May 1989, shortly before his brief marriage to Mandy Smith. He named it **Sticky Fingers** after a Stones' album. The walls contain mementos of the Stones' career from

Wyman's extensive collection, but not the zimmer frame that comedian Spike Milligan gave him as a wedding present.

Fleetwood Mac drummer Mick Fleetwood lived at 74d Kensington High Street in 1968, at the time the band released their eponymous debut album. Led Zeppelin guitarist Jimmy Page bought the Gothic-styled **Tower House** at 29 Melbury Road from the Irish actor Richard Harris in April 1974. Page, an Aleister Crowley fanatic, redecorated the place with satanic symbols. Underground film-maker Kenneth Anger lived in the basement while editing his film *Lucifer Rising*. The more mainstream director, Michael Winner, was Page's next door neighbour and Winner asked him if he would compose the soundtrack to *Deathwish II*. Page agreed and came up with a memorable score, which is more than can be said for the film itself.

Above: *Sticky Fingers* was an album for the Rolling Stones and then a Kensington restaurant financed by Bill Wyman.

All the big names of punk played early gigs at the **Nashville Rooms** at 171 North End Road, an upstairs room in a massive pub near the Cromwell Road. Today, the room is unrecognizable and has been swallowed up by an anonymous pub the size of Coventry. It started out as a country and western music venue and later became inextricably linked with the emergence of the London punk scene in 1977. Early gigs were played by the Stranglers and Eddie and the Hot Rods (none of them were actually called Eddie), another raw rhythm and blues group who, like Dr Feelgood, straddled pub rock and punk. They played their first London gig at the Nashville in May 1975 and were signed to Island Records after being spotted here.

The Nashville was famous for early appearances by Elvis Costello and the Sex Pistols, who supported Joe Strummer's pre-Clash band the 101ers, but before too long the line-up was the other way round. The Sex Pistols inspired Strummer to quit his group and form the Clash. It was also at the Nashville that the final line-up of the Damned (formerly called London SS) was completed when drummer Rat Scabies and bassist Captain Sensible (real name Ray Burns) met vocalist Dave Vanian. A Buddy Holly lookalike called Declan MacManus made his live debut at the Nashville on 27 May 1977, not long after he had been renamed Elvis Costello by Stiff Records' manager, Jake Riviera – his own name changed from Andrew Jakeman by deed poll. Much later in his career Costello went to Nashville to record his country music album, *Almost Blue*, but this time it was the real Nashville, home of country music, in Tennessee, USA.

The **Kensington** in Russell Gardens became a regular pub rock venue in the 1970s with frequent performances by Brinsley Schwarz, Ducks Deluxe and Kilburn and the High Roads. Eddie and

Above: The hirsute early days of Queen, not a garage band from Garageland – more like a college band from Collegeland.

the Hot Rods secured their first gig at the Kensington through high-energy rockers Dr Feelgood.

The last home of late Queen frontman Freddie Mercury is barely visible behind a garden wall shrine of ink and spraypaint, daubed by adoring fans from all over the world. In 1980, Mercury bought **1 Logan Place**, off Kensington High Street for £500,000, but didn't actually move in until the mid-1980s. He lived there until his death in November 1991, a skeletal echo of his former flamboyant self. Logan Place is not far from 12 Stafford Terrace, where Mercury had lived before. Set in an acre of mature landscaped gardens and hidden behind high brick walls,

Garden Lodge gave Mercury almost total privacy. The elegant Kensington home had previously belonged to the Hoare banking family and the play on words was not lost on Mercury. He wasted little time rechristening his new home the Whore House. After Queen's last performance at Knebworth, in August 1986, Mercury retired from public life and became a virtual recluse. The hero of Live Aid ended up close to Kensington High Street and the famous Biba Boutique of the 1960s, an icon of the glamorous life he craved when he fled suburban Feltham in 1966. Most shrines tend to attract loitering fans and Logan Place is no different. Some obsessive Mercury fans even write to his lifelong friend Mary Austin demanding access to the house.

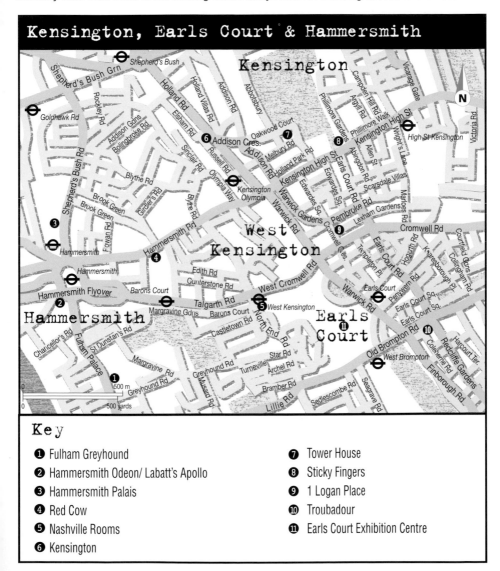

Kensington, Earls Court & Hammersmith

Key

❶ Fulham Greyhound
❷ Hammersmith Odeon/ Labatt's Apollo
❸ Hammersmith Palais
❹ Red Cow
❺ Nashville Rooms
❻ Kensington
❼ Tower House
❽ Sticky Fingers
❾ 1 Logan Place
❿ Troubadour
⓫ Earls Court Exhibition Centre

EARLS COURT

Rolling Stones' drummer Charlie Watts got his lucky musical break at the **Troubadour**, 265 Old Brompton Road, a famous coffee bar, which is still very much around today. He met blues impresario Alexis Korner here and was invited to play drums for Korner's band Blues Incorporated at both the Marquee and the Ealing Club. The Troubadour opened around 1955 and by the early 1960s was hosting live folk in its basement. In 1962, on his first visit to England, Bob Dylan performed here when he played small venues to promote his first album. It was not until his second UK trip to support *The Freewheelin' Bob Dylan* and *The Times They Are A-Changing*, that Dylan played to larger audiences. A much larger venue is the **Earls Court Exhibition Centre** nearby. The big bands play here and we're not talking the Joe Loss or Ted Heath Orchestras. In August 1980, Pink Floyd performed *The Wall*, erecting and then demolishing a huge wall on stage.

HAMMERSMITH

The first real jazz group from America to tour the UK was the Original Dixieland Jazz Band, an all-white band from New Orleans. They played at the opening of the Palais de Danse,

a new concert venue that opened at 242 Shepherd's Bush Road in October 1919. They seemed to set the scene for the US-influenced dance band mania of the 1920s. Before long the place became known as the **Hammersmith Palais**. Early on it featured real live jazz and Joe Loss and his Orchestra secured a residency here. Elvis Costello's father, Ross MacManus, worked with the Loss Orchestra as a singer and the young Declan would regularly go to watch them play. The venue has since been immortalized in the Clash's fusion of

Left: The Troubadour on Old Brompton Road was the venue for an early Bob Dylan gig.

Opposite: Earl's Court Exhibition Centre has attracted all the big players such as Led Zeppelin, Pink Floyd and Oasis.

punk and reggae 'White Man in Hammersmith Palais', Joe Strummer's tale of attending an all-night reggae concert at the Palais where he was the only white person present. At the start of the song Strummer namechecks what was presumably the line-up, representing different strands of reggae: Dillinger and Leroy Smart, Delroy Wilson and UK pop reggae's Ken Boothe who had a 1970s smash hit with 'Everything I Own'. The later lyric 'Turning rebellion into money' may well have been a swipe (perhaps even self-inflicted) at the punk movement of the time.

David Bowie moved effortlessly between rock, cabaret and psychedelia and was aided by his late guitarist Mick Ronson and loads of eyeshadow. Bowie killed off his character Ziggy Stardust at the **Hammersmith Odeon** in Queen Caroline Street, now the **Labatt's Apollo**, at the end of his UK tour in July 1973.

Opposite: Sheffield rockers Def Leppard at the Hammersmith Odeon; long, frizzy hair not compulsory but it sure helped.

Left: Divine – truly a one off – was just one of the unusual acts to hold a concert at the Hammersmith Odeon.

For years the 3,500-seat Hammersmith Odeon was one of London's top pop and rock concert venues. George Harrison met Eric Clapton here for the first time during the 1964 'Another Beatles Christmas Show'. Lord Upminster himself, Ian Dury, played his first major London concert at the Odeon in May 1978. The audience were told to prepare for 'one of the jewels in England's crown' and on came not Dury but his hero, veteran music hall star Max Wall, who was barracked by the crowd until Dury quietened them down when he reappeared with his band.

The **Fulham Greyhound**, 175 Fulham Palace Road, started as a live venue in 1971. It was soon open seven nights a week. Elvis Costello's band, before he became Elvis, was the busy Flip City. They played regular gigs on London's pub circuit including the Greyhound in April 1975.

The Police played their first London gig at the **Red Cow**, at 157 Hammersmith Road, in 1977, after noisy, no-bullshit Aussie rockers AC/DC made their UK debut the previous April. The Jam had a residency here in January 1977, shortly after their first set of gigs at the 100 Club and the Fulham Greyhound. It was at the Greyhound, in 1974, that they supported Thin Lizzy at their London debut.

SHEPHERD'S BUSH

In the early 1960s, the Who played the Goldhawk Social Club at 205 Goldhawk Road, during their first few months together. Across the road at 150 Goldhawk Road were the premises of Townhouse Studios. The Jam recorded *Setting Sons* here in October 1979. That same year Peter Gabriel recorded the first sessions for 'Games Without Frontiers', the song that launched his solo career. The Shepherd's Bush Empire remains a popular rock and pop venue today. Up until 1991 the place was the BBC TV theatre where, amongst other shows, 'Wogan' was broadcast.

Above: Shepherd's Bush Empire from 'Wogan' to heavy metal bands like Thunder.

ACTON

After the Who's Top 10 success with 'I Can't Explain' in April 1965, their schedule grew more hectic, with an ever-increasing number of TV and radio appearances. A typical week in early 1965 included a supplement to their Tuesday night Marquee slot with gigs at west London venues such as Acton's **White Hart Hotel** at 264 High Street.

Singer Adam Faith lived at 4 Churchfield Road East while attending John Perring Junior and Acton Wells Schools.

By spring of 1976, Mick Jones' pre-Clash band, London SS, had fizzled out and a brand new group featuring Mick, Paul Simonon, and guitarist Keith Levene began rehearsing at a first floor squat at 22 Davis Road, Acton.

Three members of the Who attended **Acton County Grammar School** in Gunnersbury Lane between the late 1950s and 1961. Roger Daltrey, a year above John Entwistle and Pete Townshend, was expelled in 1960 because he refused to wear his school uniform. He asked Entwistle and Townshend to join his band the Detours in 1962. Ian Gillan, singer with Deep Purple, was also a pupil at the school.

EALING

You know what blues musicians are like. They're too much into their music to bother about simple things like thinking up sexy club names. This certainly was the case with the famed **Ealing Club**, at 42a The Broadway, in the early 1960s. While it was hardly the most imaginatively-named nightspot, it didn't matter because it became London's first regular rhythm and

Acton & Ealing

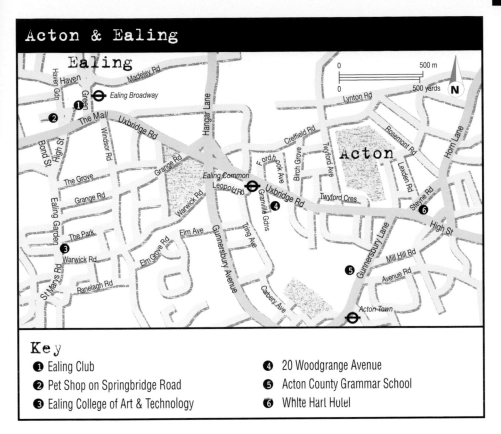

Key

1 Ealing Club

2 Pet Shop on Springbridge Road

3 Ealing College of Art & Technology

4 20 Woodgrange Avenue

5 Acton County Grammar School

6 White Hart Hotel

blues venue and provided some early gigs for the Rolling Stones. Mick and the boys played here over 20 times between July 1962 and February 1963. Early ticket flyer directions were equally uncomplicated: 'Ealing Broadway station, turn left, cross at zebra, go down steps between ABC teashop and jewellers.' The same directions apply today, but you won't find a teashop or a live music club. The site is now the home of the tantalizingly called Club Azure and there's precious little blues played here.

The Ealing Club originally opened in January 1959 as a jazz dive and was soon nicknamed the Moist Hoist because of its position in a leaky basement at the foot of some steep external steps. Condensation poured down the walls and dripped incessantly from the ceiling when the club was full, threatening to electrocute musicians and audience alike. Guitarist Alexis Korner, a musician who was massively influential in the spread of blues in England, wanted the place as a regular gig for his own band, Blues Incorporated. And soon after he opened the Ealing Club in March 1962, it attracted every budding guitarist or harmonica player for miles. Through Blues Incorporated he met the Rolling Stones. It was here that Brian Jones first introduced himself to Mick Jagger and Keith Richards. Early Blues Incorporated gigs featured singer Art Wood (Ronnie's brother), drummer Charlie Watts, the young Brian Jones (then known as Elmo Lewis) and an unknown Chuck Berry fan called Mick Jagger, who brought along his old Dartford schoolfriend, Keith Richards. Soon enough Charlie Watts understood why the club got its nickname. As drummer, he sat directly underneath the pavement light from the street above, from which dripped water down his neck and all over the drums, making the skins stretch. Next day, the band rebuilt the stage and suspended a tarpaulin across it. The tarpaulin caught the water but played hell with the acoustics. In May 1962, Blues Inc transferred from the Ealing Club to the Marquee (see Oxford Street) for a regular Thursday night slot that featured new recruits to the band, including Jack Bruce on bass and Ginger Baker on drums.

In 1964, Pete Townshend of the Who lived in the rented flat above his parents' house at **20 Woodgrange Avenue**, near Ealing Common. While living here he perfected the distinctive power-chord technique that started the group's first hit 'I Can't Explain'. He'd just left art school on St Mary's Road and shared the flat with his old art school pal Richard Barnes (later an author of books about the Who). While living there, Townshend would stay up all night talking to his friend about what the band meant and where it was going. When Townshend tried to make a recording studio by soundproofing the floor with concrete, the ceiling started to collapse and his parents kicked him out.

Queen of the suburbs – that's the nickname for the leafy West London suburb of Ealing, not Neil Tennant of the Pet Shop Boys. However, the pop duo, which he started with Chris Lowe, was named after some friends who worked in a pet shop on **Springbridge Road**, just off Ealing Broadway.

Ealing College of Art and Technology on St Mary's Road boasts alumni such as Ronnie Wood, David Bowie, Pete Townshend and Freddie Mercury. For fine art, it was usually the place you went before going on to postgraduate work at the Slade, Chelsea or the Royal College of Art. Once ensconced in the Who, manager Kit Lambert encouraged Townshend's stage violence as a form of auto-destructive art – a concept Townshend was exposed to at Ealing Art School via lectures by Gustav Metzger. The artist became a Who fan and went to some of their shows. Later in the decade, Freddie Mercury studied for a diploma in graphic art and design at Ealing, arriving in September 1966 as a mature student of 20.

GREENFORD

The Who drummer Keith Moon launched his career with the group at the Oldfield Hotel pub, Oldfield Lane, in early 1964 in extraordinary circumstances. It must have been a scary vision for the rest of the band. While playing a gig, the Who were approached mid-set by a drunken Moon, who leaped on stage declaring in no uncertain terms that he could do better than their drummer. Dressed totally in an orange outfit, Moon was allowed on stage by other members of the Who who let him try out on the drums. They discovered that he was true to his word and offered him the job. The band pioneered their trademark electronic feedback sound at later Oldfield gigs with their new Marshall Amps.

Opposite: ... and it's Pete Townshend by a nose! Garish gear was order of the day for the Who's early gigs.

SOUTH WEST

Elvis Costello didn't want to go there, but the King's Road has always been at the cutting edge of fashion. From Mary Quant's Bazaar boutique to McLaren and Westwood's shop Sex. Nearby, is the locale of the Small Faces' chaotic flat in Pimlico and Battersea Power Station, used on a Pink Floyd album cover. And you thought pigs couldn't fly! South-west is home to the Royal Albert Hall – not just a classical venue. Further afield Marc Bolan met his maker and in Richmond, the site of one of London's weirdest venues, the late Eel Pie Island, can be found.

Ex-Velvet Underground's John Cale standing under an aptly named street in Chelsea.

BUCKINGHAM PALACE

What better spot for a publicity stunt than outside the picturesque central London location of Britain's most important royal address? The Sex Pistols' famously short-lived signing to A&M Records took place on a table outside the front gates of **Buckingham Palace** on 10 March 1977. Through the label, the band released their first single, 'God Save The Queen', their alternative take on the Queen's Silver Jubilee celebrations. The record was banned from the BBC playlists, but with a beautiful irony it topped the UK charts, although the BBC somehow managed to

Below: The Sex Pistols sign to A&M in front of Buckingham Palace. Their association lasted even less time than a royal marriage.

Belgravia, South Kensington, Chelsea & Pimlico

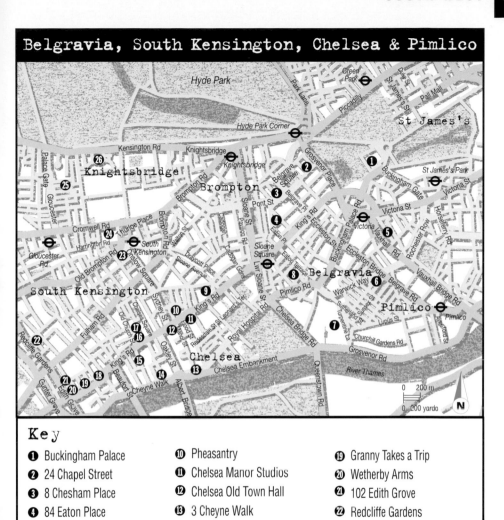

Key

- ❶ Buckingham Palace
- ❷ 24 Chapel Street
- ❸ 8 Chesham Place
- ❹ 84 Eaton Place
- ❺ Axfords
- ❻ 79a Warwick Square
- ❼ 22 Westmoreland Terrace
- ❽ 20 Ebury Street
- ❾ Bazaar
- ❿ Pheasantry
- ⓫ Chelsea Manor Studios
- ⓬ Chelsea Old Town Hall
- ⓭ 3 Cheyne Walk
- ⓮ 48 Cheyne Walk
- ⓯ Sound Techniques Studio
- ⓰ 36a Old Church Street
- ⓱ 44 Old Church Street
- ⓲ Sex
- ⓳ Granny Takes a Trip
- ⓴ Wetherby Arms
- ㉑ 102 Edith Grove
- ㉒ Redcliffe Gardens
- ㉓ 4 Old Brompton Road
- ㉔ Cromwellian
- ㉕ Blaises
- ㉖ Royal Albert Hall

position it at no. 2. Less than a week after the A&M signing, the record company cancelled the contract, but the Sex Pistols retained their £75,000 advance.

Back in October 1965, the Beatles were far more gracious to Her Majesty when they went to Buckingham Palace to receive their MBEs. Perhaps they should have performed 'Get Back' in support of police outside who struggled to control the hordes of fans. Not everyone supported the Fabs' investiture: one stuffy MBE holder complained that the British royal family had now reduced him to the same level as 'a bunch of vulgar numbskulls'. John Lennon later returned his MBE to the Queen, in November 1969, as a protest against British involvement in the Nigeria–Biafra war and the country's political support of American involvement in Vietnam. More recently, Bob Geldof was knighted here in 1986 and Paul McCartney in 1997.

BELGRAVIA

In early 1965, the Who's managers Kit Lambert and Chris Stamp moved to **84 Eaton Place** in the heart of opulent Belgravia after a run-in with the bailiffs. Lambert installed Pete Townshend in a flat above the office along with a couple of Revox tape machines and encouraged him to start writing. Townshend came up with 'My Generation', hoping he died before he got old: Townshend didn't but plenty of others have. Pete Townshend also lived at **8 Chesham Place** where he hung a Union Jack flag which became the group's emblem. Rolling Stone Brian Jones also lived in Chesham Place in early 1968.

Beatles' manager Brian Epstein lived at **24 Chapel Street**, off Belgrave Square, his main London home, bought in December 1964. Epstein was found dead here on 27 August 1967 after an overdose of pills. He was aged just 32 and his death, during the 'Summer of Love', came as a bitter shock to many. Three months earlier, in May 1967 at Epstein's launch party for the release of 'Sgt Pepper', Paul McCartney met American photographer and future wife Linda Eastman. The couple had met briefly at the Bag O'Nails Club in Kingly Street a few days previously.

SOUTH KENSINGTON and KENSINGTON GORE

First opened in 1871, as a memorial to Queen Victoria's husband, the glass-domed oval of the **Royal Albert Hall** on Kensington Gore is one of London's most instantly recognizable landmarks and is the site of the annual summer promenade concerts, which culminate in patriotic hordes waving Union flags. For over 40 years, the Albert Hall has also been a leading rock music venue. Janis Joplin's UK debut was here, and when Bob Dylan and his band the Hawks (later to become more famous as the Band) appeared here in May 1966 and plugged in their amplifiers on stage, they were greeted by some famously hostile audiences. Dylan's decision to depart from his acoustic roots and play electric instruments for the first time was barracked with a cry of 'Judas!'

The Everly Brothers chose the Albert Hall as the venue for their reunion concert in September 1984. Cream said farewell here at their final concert in November 1968, splitting after less than two years together, but Eric Clapton did not say goodbye to the venue forever. Since 1989, this magnificent 5,000-seat circular venue has hosted Clapton's annual concerts. Paul McCartney met his future fiancée, Jane Asher, at a Beatles BBC radio concert in April 1963.

A budding actress, Asher was captured by a *Radio Times* photographer screaming her appreciation for the Beatles. The hall's classical heritage has inspired some unlikely visitors: in September 1969, Deep Purple recorded their *Concerto For Group And Orchestra* with the Royal Philharmonic Orchestra. In January 1982, Elvis Costello and the Attractions headlined here, also with the Royal Philharmonic in tow.

In the autumn of 1966, Jimi Hendrix mesmerized audiences when he played guitar with his teeth at **Blaises** nightclub. It was one of Hendrix's early London gigs with the Experience (Mitch Mitchell and Noel Redding) and he was cheered on by Ronnie Wood and friends. Blaises was another mid-1960s upmarket club situated in the basement of the Imperial Hotel at 121 Queen's Gate, which was demolished in 1992. It was another favourite nightclub of the Beatles: John Lennon and George Harrison saw the Byrds here in August 1965 and Paul McCartney came to see Jimi Hendrix in 1967.

After increased drug dependency and erratic behaviour hastened his departure from Pink Floyd in 1968, Syd Barrett moved into a flat in Egerton Court, a mansion block at **4 Old Brompton Road**, opposite South Kensington tube station. The flat belonged to Storm Thorgersen who designed album covers for the Floyd. It was here that Barrett was put in a linen cupboard by his mates when experiencing a bad trip.

CROMWELL ROAD

Rock's most famous acid casualty, Syd Barrett, shared a two-storey flat at 101 Cromwell Road, now demolished. He moved here in 1968 when he broke with Pink Floyd. He hung out with various characters and acid missionaries, experimenting with drugs; among the group was a psychotic character called Scotty who apparently spiked everything. Barrett and his cronies never had a cup of tea or a glass of water unless they got it from the tap themselves and even then they'd still be worried.

When the Who smashed their equipment on stage, their manager Kit Lambert had to foot the bill. To pay for it, he often took to gambling at the **Cromwellian**, a three-storey Victorian building with a dance club and casino upstairs at 3 Cromwell Road, opposite the Natural History Museum. 'I used to watch him do it,' recalled Who bassist John Entwistle. 'I'd be there with my £20 wages and see him blow several hundred quid. Sometimes he'd actually win.' The Cromwellian billed itself as 'Three floors of fun in Royal Kensington' and often featured big-name groups and pirate station DJs in the basement, as well as the gambling parlour on the top floor. Soon after opening, the Crom started booking top US and rhythm and blues acts including Soloman Burke and Doris Troy. Later, Swinging London swung by in 1967: the Beatles visited often that year. The Cromwellian was renamed 3rd Street in the late 1980s and is now the CM Casino.

CHELSEA

KING'S ROAD

While Elvis Costello didn't want to go to Chelsea (he resented the place enough to write a sarcastic song about it in 1978), thousands of rock fans do, and continue to traipse its streets in search of places linked to their musical heroes. The King's Road has always been a catwalk where the latest fashions are paraded but it is also a place for teenagers to hang out and define themselves by the type of music they listen to. When punk arrived in the mid-1970s, it challenged the complacency of the supergroups and stuck a firm two fingers up at tired stadium rock dinosaurs like Emerson, Lake and Palmer and their drawn-out concept albums. Punk gave foreign tourists something else to photograph along the King's Road other than the Chelsea pensioners, strolling proudly along in their red great coats.

The cradle of punk was a clothes shop at 430 King's Road selling Teddy Boy outfits and bondage trousers, owned by art school rebel Malcolm McLaren and Vivienne Westwood. They took over the shop in 1971, originally calling it Let It Rock, specializing in 1950s rock'n'roll clothing. The shop later became Too Fast To Live Too Young To Die. When McLaren visited New York in 1973 he became embroiled in the emerging Big Apple punk scene and went on to manage the New York Dolls. On his return, he drew inspiration from Richard Hell's fashionable ripped T-shirts and in 1974 relaunched the shop as **Sex**, a name the *Daily Mirror* found so disturbing they started a campaign to close it down. McLaren and Westwood pioneered the look that proved so influential in punk's formative years: spiky hair, clothes joined together with safety pins and ripped shirts worn by kids from Basingstoke to Burnley. Using regular customers, McLaren formed a band just to promote the shop. Bassist Glen Matlock was hired as were two school friends, drummer Paul Cook and guitarist Steve Jones who hung out in his shop. When he was unable to convince Richard Hell or Midge Ure to join the band, McLaren auditioned a green-haired Sex regular named John Lydon (Johnny Rotten) by having him sing the Alice Cooper classic 'School's Out', backed by the jukebox in the nearby pub, the Roebuck. Rotten was hired for his attitude rather than vocal range. The Sex

Opposite: Johnny Rotten of the Sex Pistols epitomized punk and its blatant lack of respect for the establishment.

> ❝ I liked the name very much. I thought it was hilarious. The word 'sex' had never been used in that blatant way before and to put it into a pop band was very funny. I thought it was perfect to offend old ladies. ❞

JOHN LYDON ON THE NAMING OF THE SEX PISTOLS

Pistols were born. In February 1977, despite a glaringly obvious lack of any musical ability, Sid Vicious joined the band.

Chrissie Hynde of the Pretenders and Clash manager Bernie Rhodes both worked at the shop in the mid-1970s. Sex became Seditionaries in 1976 and a brass plaque on the door read: 'Clothes for Heroes'. With T-shirts costing £6 each, at a time when beer was 30p a pint, you needed a pretty heroic bank balance to afford one. Today 430 King's Road is still a clothes shop, a boutique called World's End.

Glen Matlock (who, according to Johnny Rotten, was sacked from the Sex Pistols for 'admitting liking the Beatles') would no doubt approve of the many rock legends' associations with Chelsea. In 1967, Eric Clapton lived in part of a warren for artists and musicians known

as the **Pheasantry**, 152 King's Road. His neighbour was Australian artist Martin Sharpe of *Oz* magazine. Sharpe also designed the day-glo cover for the Cream album *Disraeli Gears* as well as *Wheels of Fire*. Clapton penned Cream classics 'Badge' and 'Sunshine of Your Love' while living there. It's now the premises of a well-known pizza chain.

Nearby is **Chelsea Old Town Hall**, 169 King's Road, the venue in July 1969 for the launch of John Lennon and Yoko Ono's first single 'Give Peace a Chance'. The couple did not attend the event themselves, having been hospitalized in Scotland after a car crash, but Ringo Starr stepped in.

Rolling Stones' bassist Bill Wyman first auditioned for the band in their regular rehearsal room at 500 King's Road, the **Wetherby Arms** (now a restaurant, imaginatively named '500'), in December 1962. Originally Wyman was deemed too old for the band but he was hired because the other Stones liked his car and were impressed by his amplifiers.

Below & opposite: McLaren and Westwood's shop Sex, now called World's End.

Clothes are inextricably linked with music and fashion designer Mary Quant was largely responsible for placing the King's Road at the epicentre of Swinging London. She opened her **Bazaar** boutique on the King's Road (now a coffee bar), on the corner of Markham Square, in 1955 with her husband Alexander Plunket Greene. She became the Emmeline Pankhurst of ladies fashion, liberating women from the straitjacket of stuffy long skirts and cardigans with innovative designs. With high fashion brought to the masses, modern girls no longer had to dress like their mothers. Rolling Stones' manager Andrew Oldham later

Below: Models show off the fab gear on offer at the boutique Hung on You. The girl holds a requisite copy of the Stones' *Aftermath* released in 1966.

Above: Mary Quant and her designs available from Bazaar. Hers was the first boutique to open on the King's Road.

turned up at Bazaar and talked himself into a job. 'At first fashion was the fashion, then fashion became the music,' he explained. Bazaar was such a success that it would sell out of new collections before Quant could finish dressing the window.

By the late 1960s the King's Road had become a fashion institution. You were quite likely to run into Mick Jagger buying clothes in the groovy **Granny Takes a Trip** at 488 Kings Road, a shop that stocked seriously psychedelic clothes, which was also popular with Pink Floyd, T Rex and the Faces. Or you might spot Jimi Hendrix rummaging for antique shirts and coats in Chelsea Antiques Market. There was also Quorum, where Pink Floyd's David Gilmour used to work. He quit his day job driving a delivery truck when he was asked to join the Floyd in January 1968. Today the King's Road seems to have been neutralized, looking pretty much the same as any other high street in Britain, a monotonous line of well-known brands like Boots, the Body Shop and Pizza Hut. The chain gang's all here; they've just been reshuffled in a different order.

Above: Def Leppard's guitarist, Steve Clark, died in Chelsea in 1991.

OLD CHURCH STREET

Old Slowhand Eric Clapton moved back to his Chelsea pad at **36a Old Church Street** in 1992 after selling his Surrey mansion Hurtwood Edge. A few doors along, at 46a Old Church Street, is the site of the former **Sound Techniques Studio** where Pink Floyd recorded their first single, 'Arnold Layne', in February 1967. A bigger hit, 'See Emily Play', was laid down here three months later. Written by Syd Barrett, it reached number six in the charts in 1967. The song was inspired by the sculptor Emily Young, the daughter of Lord Kennet. She was a pupil at Holland Park comprehensive along with her best friend, actress Anjelica Huston. In her teenage years she was an enthusiastic hippy and a regular at the psychedelic UFO club and her style was immortalized in the lyric 'wearing a gown that touches the ground'.

London's rock landscape is litterered with drug-fuelled premature deaths and Chelsea has not escaped. In January 1991, Steve Clark, the guitarist with British heavy metal band Def Leppard, died of an overdose of drugs and alcohol in his flat at **44 Old Church Street**. The Sheffield group were at the height of their commercial success having released the album *Hysteria*.

FLOOD STREET

Chelsea Manor Studios at 1–11 Flood Street will be forever remembered as the place where the Beatles were photographed for the album cover of *Sgt Pepper's Lonely Hearts Club Band* on 30 March 1967. It was in Studio Four with photographer Michael Cooper. The band was photographed in front of a remarkable collage designed by Peter Blake and posed for the other shots that appear on the inner sleeves that same evening. Studio 4 is now a classroom for make-up artists, but Studios Two and Three are still used for photography.

CHEYNE WALK

At one stage in the late 1960s, it seemed that most of the Rolling Stones lived somewhere along fashionable Cheyne Walk. At **3 Cheyne Walk** was Keith Richards' pad. He lived there during the late 1960s in a mansion overlooking the Thames and shared the place with girlfriend Anita Pallenburg. In 1967, Mick Jagger paid £40,000 and moved in at **48 Cheyne Walk**. Both Jagger's girlfriend, Marianne Faithfull, who met Mick at a party held at 100 Cheyne Walk and future wife Bianca Jagger lived with him at this address but obviously not at the same time. Many Stones' songs were written in the studio he built in the garden.

The lyrics to 'A Day In The Life' by the Beatles were inspired by an actual event in West Brompton. On the night of 17 December 1966 their friend, 21-year-old heir to the Guinness fortune Tara Browne, was killed instantly when he crashed his Lotus Elan while on LSD. He hit the back of a parked car in **Redcliffe Gardens**. A few days later, John Lennon wrote the song after reading the newspaper account of a car crash at some traffic lights.

Talk about a crowded house. Between 1962 and 1963, Mick Jagger, Brian Jones and Keith Richards shared a flat in the more bohemian end of Chelsea. Jones lived in the middle floor flat at **102 Edith Grove** when the Rolling Stones first formed, with Jagger and Richards moving in later. The Beatles even attended a party at the flat in April 1963, after seeing the Stones play live at the Crawdaddy club in Richmond. They stayed until 4 a.m. Some hardcore Stones' fans believe Edith Grove was the place where the band were formed and they have asked English Heritage to consider erecting a blue plaque at the house.

Below: Not all of the Rolling Stones lived in Cheyne Walk. Here they appear to be doing their 'Man at C&A' fashion spread.

DECCA

PIMLICO

Above: The Who's rock opera *Tommy*. It was later made in to a film.

A chatty cleaner called Marge provided the inspiration for the 'How's your Bert's lumbago?' line in the Small Faces' 'Lazy Sunday Afternoon'. She worked at **22 Westmoreland Terrace** when the band rented the house in 1965. They wrote songs here, sometimes on the upstairs toilet, as it was often the only place that offered any peace and quiet. The house swelled with hedonistic abandon: 24-hour parties and teenage girls camped outside the front door. The group's Ronnie Lane, Steve Marriott and Ian McLagan lived there for a year, but not drummer Kenney Jones who moved out early on. It was also a popular hang-out for others in the music business and Beatles' manager Brian Epstein had his first LSD trip there.

The band's organist Ian McLagan recalls one occasion when Brian Epstein and Moody Blues' drummer Graeme Edge dropped in: 'When Ronnie [Lane] found me, I'd been spinning in the egg chair for some time, the room rotating slowly around me. He thought it would be a good idea to go for a walk. There was no one else on the street, it was silent except for our footsteps as we walked down Westmoreland Terrace into Lupus Street, and across Grosvenor Road to the Thames Embankment. Across the river, one of Battersea Power Station's four brick chimneys belched out what might have looked like smoke on any other morning, but we were witnessing the birth of the universe. The effects of the acid might have eased off just a little, but not enough for us not to recognize the history of all life written in a puff of smoke above the glistening Thames.'

David Bowie's first manager Ralph Horton, also of the Moody Blues, lived at **79a Warwick Square**. Bowie himself lived here for a few months in the mid-1960s, when he wrote some of his earliest songs. With Horton's help, Bowie changed his name from David Jones to David Bowie. He was worried about confusion with Davy Jones from the Monkees, so he borrowed the surname from Jim Bowie, a fighter with Davy Crockett at the Alamo. The name Bowie, he reckoned, would also cut through to the truth.

Pete Townshend wrote much of the rock opera *Tommy* when he lived on the top floor at **20 Ebury Street** between 1967–68. He soundproofed the flat so it could be used as a studio.

VAUXHALL

The late Ian Dury overcame childhood polio to become one of the most charismatic and long-lasting stars of the punk era. For the cover of his memorable 1977 album *New Boots And Panties!!*, Dury posed with his son, Baxter, outside a shop called **Axfords** at 306 Vauxhall Bridge Road, now long departed. The album, which included 'Billericay Dickie' and 'Clever Trevor', glorified East End rhyming slang, sold more than a million copies and remained in the album chart for the next two years, giving Stiff Records some much needed economic stability. At this time, Dury lived in Vauxhall in a block of flats, next to the Cricketeers pub, called Oval Mansions at Kennington Oval, which he nicknamed Catshit Mansions. Dury's home was a £3-a-week bedsit on the fifth floor overlooking the Oval Cricket Ground. It was here that he wrote early Blockheads lyrics. The Who played the Oval in September 1971, supported by America and the Faces.

BATTERSEA

One of London's most instantly recognizable landmarks – not Jeffrey Archer's face but **Battersea Power Station** – was used as a backdrop in the Beatles film *Help* and the Who's second rock opera *Quadrophenia*. It is best remembered for adorning the cover of Pink Floyd's *Animals* – albeit with a huge 40-foot inflatable pig dominating the scene. During the shoot in December 1976, the porcine prop broke free from its moorings and airline pilots suddenly reported seeing an UFP (Unidentified Flying Pig). It caused disruption and air traffic control had to re-route all the flights over the south of England. The pig was last seen being eaten by the French.

Below: Ian Dury and his son pose for the cover of his *New Boots and Panties!* album.

The Who recorded *Quadrophenia* a stone's throw from Battersea Power Station, at **Ramport Studios**, 115-117 Thessaly Road, a former church which they had converted. Their *Odds and Sods* album cover was also photographed here.

Top British bluesman Alexis Korner supplied the rock band Free with their name after he saw them play

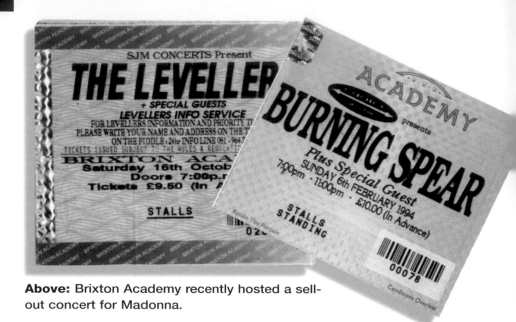

Above: Brixton Academy recently hosted a sell-out concert for Madonna.

their first gig in 1968 at the former Blue Horizon Club, 205 York Road.

It's been said that the Stranglers were the odd men out of punk. No other punk band had an organ player and certainly no punk dreamt of having a moustache. While the Clash called for political uprising and the Sex Pistols for destruction, starting with the monarchy, the Stranglers lived up to their reputation as dirty old men. In mid-September 1978 they performed 'Nice 'n' Sleazy' on stage in Battersea Park, assisted by a coterie of French strippers.

BRIXTON

Before they were famous, Status Quo used to rehearse in a room above the **George IV** pub on Streatham Hill, perfecting their new sound. Apparently the landlord was stone deaf and, according to one long-suffering regular, the venue continues the no-nonsense boogie approach by featuring crap heavy metal bands several nights a week.

Bryan Ferry, the driving force behind Roxy Music, named his group after an old cinema in Brixton called the Roxy, now closed down. David Bowie was born and spent his early childhood years in Brixton, at **40 Stansfield Road**. Under his real name David Jones, he went to nearby Stockwell Infants School on Stockwell Road. Don't bother looking for a blue plaque – there ain't one.

Brixton's former sixties **Ram Jam** club, at 390 Brixton Road, took its name from soul legend Geno Washington and the Ram Jam Band. The venue opened in February 1966 with a gig headlined by the Animals, but regular shows there reflected the ethnic mix of the area and were largely black-orientated, with Washington himself often in evidence at the venue. Dexy's

Battersea & Brixton

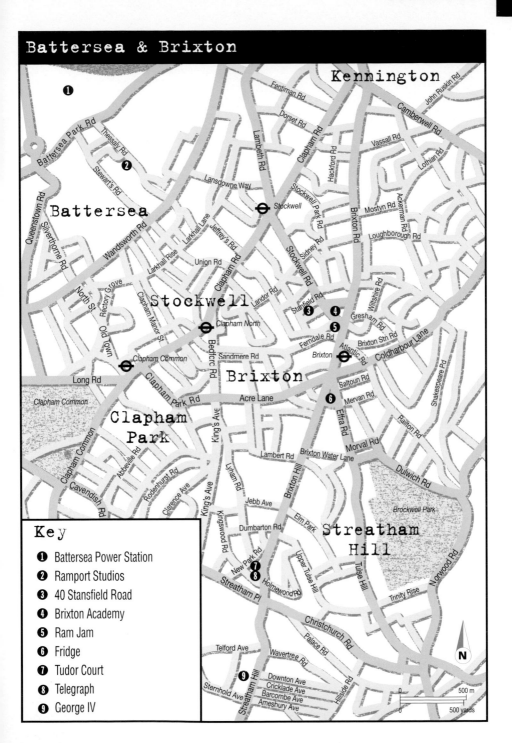

Key

❶ Battersea Power Station

❷ Ramport Studios

❸ 40 Stansfield Road

❹ Brixton Academy

❺ Ram Jam

❻ Fridge

❼ Tudor Court

❽ Telegraph

❾ George IV

Midnight Runners had a number one hit in 1980 with 'Geno', written in homage to the soul star, who is still going strong today.

When Nick Cave moved back to London in 1984, he cocooned himself for a few months in **Tudor Court** on Brixton Hill, a block of flats which had its own swimming pool. Each morning when other residents left for work, they would be greeted by the wonderful spectacle of Cave crashed out on a sunlounger by the pool wearing only a pair of leather trousers and sunglasses. In September 1974, Joe Strummer's 101ers played their first gig at the **Telegraph** pub at 228 Brixton Hill.

Brixton currently hosts two of London's hottest club and rock venues – the **Fridge** in Town Hall Parade and the **Brixton Academy** at 211 Stockwell Road. 2001 saw the Academy host Madonna's sell-out, one-hour concert and a tribute to the late Ian Dury.

WIMBLEDON

In the days before political correctness made such behaviour unacceptable and probably punishable by death, Queen rented Wimbledon Stadium for a day in September 1978 to film a video for their double A-side single 'Bicycle Race'/'Fat Bottomed Girls'. Some 65 naked models were hired to stage a nude bicycle race in the stadium. High street retailers Halfords, who supplied the bikes, refused to take the saddles back and insisted Queen stump up for their replacement. In retrospect, one wonders if this was a sound business move, as there are parts of surburban south London where such artifacts fetch good money. It was a scantily-clad time in London's musical history – only the previous day, the Stranglers had performed in Battersea Park assisted by strippers. Before he fronted the punk band Sham 69, Jimmy Pursey worked at Wimbledon Stadium, a few miles from Hersham in Surrey, where the band coined their name.

Marc Bolan used to live in a tiny estate of prefab council houses known as Sun Cottages, Summerstown, near Wimbledon Stadium (now demolished). Although the houses were clean, comfortable and modern, Marc described them as 'caravans with pointed roofs'. In Wimbledon he was separated from his North London friends and hated every minute of it. Earlier, Bolan left Hill Croft School in Beechcroft Road, Earlsfield, to live in central London.

Opposite and above: N.W.A. (Niggaz With Attitude) and Neneh Cherry getting into the swing of things at the Brixton Academy.

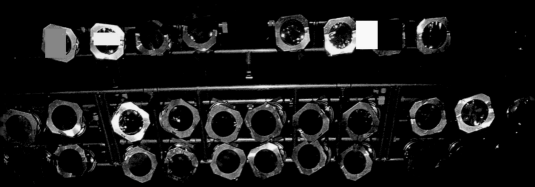

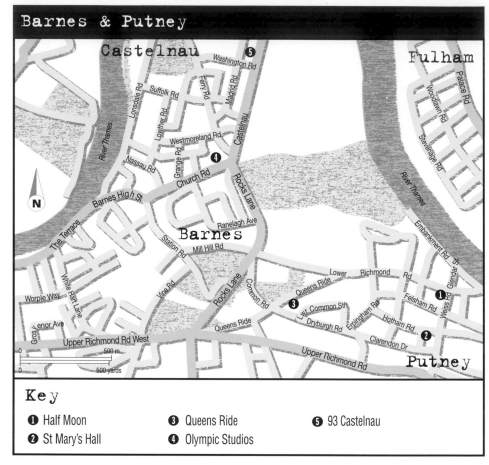

Barnes & Putney

Key

❶ Half Moon

❷ St Mary's Hall

❸ Queens Ride

❹ Olympic Studios

❺ 93 Castelnau

As the lead singer of Fairport Convention, the late Sandy Denny was central in introducing traditional folk music into the band's repertoire. The songstress was born in Worple Road, Wimbledon in 1947. She paid homage to her roots on the cover of their album *Unhalfbricking*. The cover featured no title, no band name, just a photograph of an elderly couple in front of their home with a dreamy-looking church spire in the distance. The old couple were Sandy's parents, Edna and Neil Denny, photographed a year before the album's release in 1969, outside their home on Arthur Road, Wimbledon. What originally appears to be a simple family snap is deceptive: look through the high fence and you can see members of Fairport Convention lazing around in the shade of a beech tree. You can still see elderly couples like the Dennys walking around Wimbledon: old, solid and so comfortable in each other's presence they often don't need to exchange words. For non-Fairport fans, Sandy Denny's clear, emotive voice was one of the highlights on *Led Zeppelin IV*, on which she sang a haunting duet with Robert Plant, 'The Battle of Evermore'.

A song by Bo Diddley may have given its name to Richmond's most famous rhythm and blues club, the Crawdaddy, but the great man himself once played the long-defunct Wimbledon

Palais ballroom in October 1965. Its location was on Colliers Wood High Street (formerly a furniture shop and now a new block of flats near Mill Road). In December 1963, the Beatles played a concert here at a fan club convention. The Fab Four had to perform inside a steel cage which was erected to protect them from the screaming hordes of female fans. Ah, the pressures of stardom.

BARNES

Rock stars who die before they get old are nearly always guaranteed a certain degree of lasting fame, let alone increased record sales. Fans of Marc Bolan make a pilgrimage to a tree on the humpbacked **Queens Ride** bridge in Barnes, where the White Swanster lost his life. In recent years the Performing Rights Society has erected an engraved stone dedicated to his memory. Ever since the crash, a small section of the bridge has been a Bolan shrine, decorated with ribbons, cards, messages and memorabilia. Bolan died instantly when his purple Mini 1275 GT left the road and hit the tree. A non-driver, the singer was in the passenger seat of the car, driven by his girlfriend and mother of his son, Gloria Jones. The accident happened just before 5 a.m. on 16 September 1977 when the couple were driving back to their East Sheen home. Earlier in the evening they had been celebrating at Morton's Club in Berkeley Square. If you're intent on visiting Bolan's shrine on Queens Ride bridge, take care as this can be a busy road. Expiring here would be taking hero worship a step too far.

Below: Bolan's early death has guaranteed him cult status.

The short and rather tragic life of Fairport Convention

singer Sandy Denny ended on 21 April 1978 as a result of injuries sustained while staying at a friend's house at **93 Castelnau**, not far from Queens Ride. She fell downstairs, cut her head open and was rushed to the Atkinson Morley hospital where she lay in a coma for a week before she died of a brain haemorrage. She was just 31 years old and is buried at Putney Vale Cemetery.

It's not all doom and gloom in Barnes. A happier musical milestone is the phenomenally successful **Olympic Studios** at 117 Church Road, where some truly classic albums have been recorded. Since it opened in 1968, Olympic has maintained its enviable reputation as one of the best equipped studios in the country, which is why Pulp, Bjork, Eric Clapton and the Spice Girls have been recent visitors. Built in 1906 as the Barnes Theatre, Olympic was an independently-owned London recording venue, thoughout the 1960s, frequented by the Beatles. It's now owned by EMI and has undergone extensive refurbishments. Eric Clapton made his first recording here when he played with the Yardbirds in February 1964 and subsequently recorded with Blind Faith and Derek and the Dominos.

The studios could be called Classic-Singles-R-Us. The Yardbirds' breakthrough single, 'For Your Love', was recorded here in February 1965. The Troggs' 'Wild Thing' was cut in April 1966 and in the summer of 1967 'Itchycoo Park' was taped by the Small Faces. Olympic Studios was virtually a second home for the Rolling Stones in the late 1960s and many of their classic albums were mixed here, including *Sticky Fingers* and *Let It Bleed*. One of their most enduring songs, 'Jumpin' Jack Flash', began life by chance in March 1968. While waiting for Jagger and Richards to arrive, Bill Wyman filled the time by experimenting on the piano. When Keith Richards arrived, he liked what Wyman was playing and it became the basis of the song. When the Stones weren't recording, there were plenty of other stars queuing up to get in. The legendary Glyn Johns produced the third Small Faces' album *A Nod's As Good As A Wink To A Blind Horse*. The first few tracks of Hendrix's *Electric Ladyland* was recorded here before production went to New York. Led Zeppelin recorded their first and fourth albums here. Prior to their first, they were originally called the New Yardbirds until Keith Moon suggested Lead Zeppelin – he believed they would sink faster than a lead balloon.

PUTNEY

Bill Wyman's debut with the Rolling Stones took place at **St Mary's Hall** on Hotham Road in December 1962. The hall was an early venue for the Detours and later the Who. They played here a few times in early 1963, supporting Willesden boy Johnny Kidd and the Pirates, a band who were a huge influence on drummer Keith Moon and one of their songs supplied Dr Feelgood with their name. Later, the Detours supported no less than the Rolling Stones. During their set Pete Townshend was transfixed by Keith Richards' guitar playing, particularly his rotating right arm action when he struck chords. Townshend exaggerated this and made it into his own trademark windmill, his arm whirling across the strings.

In years gone by you might have seen the Rolling Stones, the Police, Status Quo or Dire Straits play at the long-established **Half Moon**, 93 Lower Richmond Road, and even today it features live bands seven nights a week, be it blues, rock, folk and reggae. Putney's Half Moon

Above: Gloria Jones with Marc Bolan, who lived and died in south-west London. They had a son called Rolan Bolan.

is similar to many established pub venues in London, a large Edwardian pub given over to live music. The traditional pub, situated at the front, is populated by old, smirking regulars who aren't the least bit interested in rock music. It gives way to a back room where the music happens.

EAST SHEEN

On the night he died, Bolan and his girlfriend Gloria Jones were returning home to their house at 142 Upper Richmond Road West in East Sheen. They moved into this large Victorian house in September 1976, just a year before his death. In 1966, Marc played his first concert at the former Pontiac Club not too far away, at 200 Upper Richmond Road West.

RICHMOND

It's perhaps hard to think of this well-heeled west London surburb, with expensive house prices to match, as being the birthplace of British rhythm and blues; but the late rock historian John Platt described Richmond as Britain's own Mississippi Delta. Named after the Bo Diddley song 'Doing the Craw-Daddy', Richmond's infamous **Crawdaddy** club (1 Kew Road, now a pub-cum-wine bar) was to the Rolling Stones what Liverpool's Cavern was to the Beatles. The Stones, hotly tipped as the South of England's grittier response to the Fabs, started to attract crowds, which gathered in the backroom of this pub, then the **Station Hotel**. From the early 1950s, several jazz clubs ran at the hotel until the end of 1962 when the Crawdaddy's founder, a Russian emigre called Giorgio Gomelsky, began regular Sunday rhythm and blues evenings. Recently joined by Charlie Watts on drums, the Stones played their first date here in February 1963. Only 30 people turned up.

Below: The Wick, owned by Sir John Mills, then Ronnie Wood and Pete Townshend.

Pianist Ian Stewart was ousted from the band, early on, for looking too straight, although he continued to play on records and remained a road manager. For their first gig they earned £1 each, but more importantly they were soon offered a regular Sunday night residency, which established a loyal following. Gomelsky even got the Beatles to come and see the Stones perform at his club one Sunday evening in April 1963. The Fabs drove over from nearby Teddington Studios to see what all the commotion was about. Later that night both bands returned to the Stones' Edith Grove flat and it marked the start of a friendship of Britain's two biggest groups. George Harrison was so impressed with what he'd seen he suggested to Dick Rowe of Decca that he should sign them to the label.

Within six months of their Sunday night residency, the Stones had a minor hit with 'Come On' and their success forced Gomelsky to move out of the Station Hotel with its overcrowded back-room and relocate to the club-house of the **Richmond Athletic Ground** on Twickenham Road. By the end of 1963, the Yardbirds replaced the Stones as the Crawdaddy's resident band in its new location. In March 1964, Yardbirds' singer Keith Relf was taken ill in the smoky club and Eric Clapton asked a packed audience if anyone could play harmonica. A young Ronnie Wood stepped up to offer his services.

The Stones slipped through Gomelsky's grasp, and the Crawdaddy's founder lost out to predatory Andrew Oldham, who saw his first Rolling Stones' gig at the Crawdaddy club. He was dressed for the part: tab-collared shirt, black woollen tie, a three-piece suit and highly polished side-laced black boots.

Thin Lizzy frontman Phil Lynott lived at **184 Kew Road** with his wife Caroline (daughter of the late TV entertainer Leslie Crowther) until his death in January 1986 in Salisbury General Hospital. After Thin Lizzy broke up, Lynott had

Above: Phil Lynott lived with his wife and daughter in Richmond. The drugs and rock'n'roll lifestyle took its toll in 1986.

enjoyed a little success as a solo artist but his lifestyle suffered due to increasing drug abuse.

The **Wick**, a classic 20-room Georgian mansion just below the brow of Richmond Hill, boasts spectacular views over south England. Ronnie Wood bought the house from actor Sir John Mills in 1972 and lived here for most of the 1970s. Keith Richards was a regular guest in the cottage at the end of the garden, where he sought refuge from police raids on his Cheyne

Walk home. The basic track for the Stones' 'It's Only Rock'n'Roll (But I Like It)' was recorded here in Wood's home studio. And it was at the Wick in December 1975 that Wood's wife Chrissie was busted in a 'two-chicks-in-a bed' shocker. Wood lived here until 1996 but it is now owned by Pete Townshend who bought it for £2 million and renovated it extensively.

Just down the road, with equally good views over the Thames, is the double-fronted **Downe House**, at 116 Richmond Hill, which Mick Jagger bought in the 1990s. Before their divorce, Jagger lived here with Jerry Hall and their three children.

On Hill Rise is the former site of **L'Auberge**, a coffee bar frequented by the in-crowd. Peter Green, Eric Clapton and Rod Stewart were regular faces here.

Between 1961 and 1965, Richmond hosted the National Jazz and Blues Festival at the Richmond Athletic Ground. The first festival passed without incident, but posh locals never took to the annual invasion of beatniks and after 1965 their objections banished the event to Windsor. It later found a permanent home further along the river as the legendary Reading Festival. In 1963, Acker Bilk's audience suddenly deserted him *en masse* for a nearby marquee because the Rolling Stones had struck the opening chords to their first hit 'Come On'.

The former home of poet Alfred Lord Tennyson, **Tennyson House** at 15 Montpelier Row, has been owned by Pete Townshend for many years.

TWICKENHAM

Long gone but never forgotten, **Eel Pie Island** (off Water Lane, on the Thames at Twickenham) was one of London's most extraordinary rock landmarks. It was a club opened in 1956 by junk shop worker Arthur Chisnall in an attempt to keep local youngsters out of trouble. The venue soon started to host a succession of trad jazz acts like Ken Colyer. By the early 1960s, it switched to being a rhythm and blues club, with everyone from local heroes the Artwoods (led by Ronnie Wood's brother Art) to the Animals playing. Eel Pie boasted an impressive role call of bands. Among those who braved the ramshackle venue were the Yardbirds, Long John Baldry and the Who. Rod Stewart and the Rolling Stones served apprenticeships here and established their reputations.

Nowadays, its unusual setting may sound charming when faced with anodyne venues like Wembley Arena or the London Arena in Docklands, but structurally Eel Pie wasn't up to much. Little more than an ancient, shabby hotel and ballroom, it was virtually falling apart, with massive holes in the roof and decaying, dilapidated floorboards. Through the dressing room above the stage, bands could see everything going on directly underneath. It was also a hassle to get to, but well worth it apparently. Originally an old chain-ferry delivered musicians and punters to the island. The logistics were made easier in 1957 when a narrow and rickety footbridge was built. On the other side were two little old ladies sitting patiently awaiting the tuppence toll money. Bands still had to lug their own instruments and amps onto the island themselves, until an enterprising local man got himself a nice little earner transporting their equipment across the bridge on a Mini Moke. Stuffy locals complained and police often viewed it as 'a beatnik-infested vice den'. It enjoyed a renaissance in the late 1960s as a progressive rock club, but Eel Pie died with the rhythm and blues boom. As a music venue, it limped on until

Richmond & Twickenham

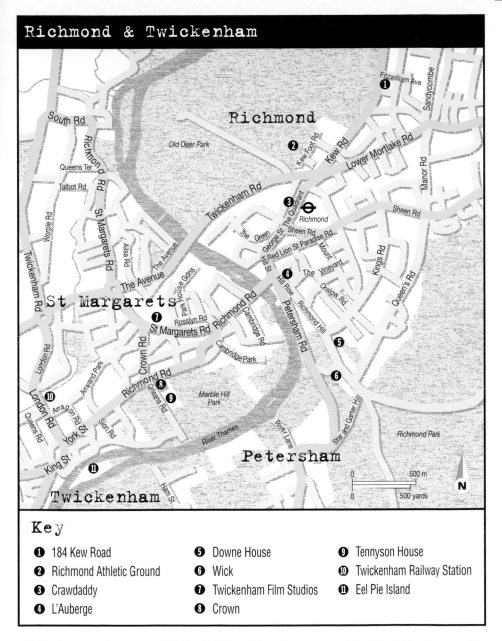

Key

❶ 184 Kew Road

❷ Richmond Athletic Ground

❸ Crawdaddy

❹ L'Auberge

❺ Downe House

❻ Wick

❼ Twickenham Film Studios

❽ Crown

❾ Tennyson House

❿ Twickenham Railway Station

⓫ Eel Pie Island

1970 when squatters occupied the building. When they were evicted the following year the premises burnt down that March in mysterious circumstances.

Nearby **Twickenham Railway Station** is not renowned for its musical leanings, but a legendary piece of rock'n'roll history took place here on 7 January 1964. It was late at night

> **Never keep your legs together when you're singing. It looks daft.**

and the blues singer Long John Baldry waited on a cold and foggy platform for the last train back to London. Baldry, a towering blues singer close to seven-foot tall, fronted the Hoochie Coochie Men, and was not short at helping out up-and-coming musicians. He had just completed a show at Eel Pie Island when he heard a wailing harmonica riff from a classic Howlin' Wolf song called 'Smokestack Lightning' at the station. The musician waiting to be discovered (and for a train) was none other than a young Brentford Football Club apprentice called Rod Stewart, who'd been to see the Eel Pie gig, and was waiting for the same train. This chance encounter became a meeting of minds. Rod Stewart said Baldry approached him and promptly made him one of his Hoochie Coochie Men as a second singer for £35 a week. He invited him to play at the Marquee club the following week. Baldry maintained he just invited Stewart along for a jam session. The two became friends and Baldry took the young singer under his wing. Stewart made his debut the following week, but not before his mother phoned up Baldry on the morning of the gig, telling him 'just make sure my son gets home on time'. Stewart's career took off with the Hoochie Coochie Men and it wasn't long before Baldry imparted his stage wisdom to his young pupil: 'Never keep your legs together when you're singing. It looks daft,' he advised.

The **Crown** at 174 Richmond Road was a Twickenham folk club that took off during the early 1960s, with Beverly Martin and Bert Jansch among the regulars. Free made an appearance later in the decade when the venue hosted blues nights.

Twickenham Film Studios, at the Barons, virtually opposite St Margaret's railway station, were used for many of the Beatles promotional films, including most of the non-location scenes in *A Hard Days Night*, *Help!* and half of *Let It Be*.

Former Genesis drummer Phil Collins's childhood home was at 78 Constance Road.

SHEPPERTON

The Warren Lodge Hotel, in Church Square, Shepperton is still a popular place for wedding receptions. The Who lived there while filming *Tommy* at Shepperton film studios. In the hotel's reception area there is a gold disc of the rock opera donated to the hotel by Roger Daltrey and dedicated to its manager. While filming, the shower heads on the walls of their bathrooms were lowered so they didn't get their hair wet when they had an early morning stage call.

Pete Townshend had trouble getting *Tommy* financed until Robert Stigwood, producer of *Saturday Night Fever* organised a $3.5 deal with Columbia Pictures. Roger Daltrey played the eponymous deaf, dumb and blind kid, but Elton John (as the Pinball Wizard) only got excited about the film when he learnt Ken Russell would be directing it. Keith Moon played Uncle Ernie but his scenes were dramatically cut when director Russell realised he couldn't act.

Above: Eel Pie Island provided an alternative place to hang out and was the venue where bands such as the Rolling Stones got started.

SOUTH EAST

Croydon's Fairfield Halls may not win prizes for architectural beauty but it has hosted a few legends in its time. And Croydon's not alone; Ziggy's spiders came from Mars, but David Bowie hailed from the suburbs of Bromley and Beckenham. South-east London seems light years away from the bright lights of Soho, but its musical influence casts its net far. Where would punk have been without Siouxsie Sioux and her Bromley contingent? Then there's Dartford, the early stamping ground for Mick Jagger and Keith Richards.

David Bowie's incarnation as Ziggy Stardust was worlds away from his birthplace in Bromley.

WATERLOO

What French tourists arriving on the Eurostar make of one of London's major railway stations being named after one of their greatest military defeats is anyone's guess. Still, **Waterloo Station** is popular with Ray Davies of the Kinks, who not only wrote a song about Terry meeting Julie there, but also wrote and starred in a TV film called *Return to Waterloo*, appearing as a busker. His 'Waterloo Sunset' was the last Kinks' track produced by Shel Talmy, a former Los Angeles studio engineer who became a top producer in the UK. Subsequently, Ray Davies produced all the Kinks' records. When he was a boy, Davies had his tonsils out at St Thomas's Hospital, close to Waterloo, on the banks of the Thames. Later, in his teenage years he crossed Waterloo Bridge every day on his way to Croydon art college. Love or loathe it, 'Waterloo Sunset' was a landmark of 1960s pop music and it captured a moment perfectly. For many, this is the quintessential London song and generations of groups that followed still rate this as one of the best pop songs ever. When Bill Haley and his Comets arrived at Waterloo Station by train from Southampton in February 1957 the rock'n' roller was besieged by adoring fans. Such a huge crowd of people met the singer that the press described Haley's arrival as the second Battle of Waterloo.

Below: Waterloo Station immortalized in the Kinks' 'Waterloo Sunset'.

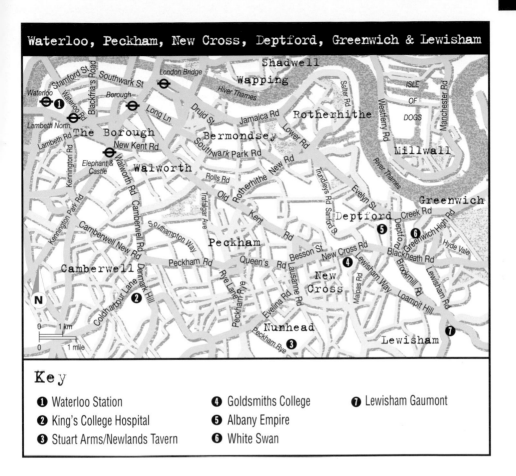

Waterloo, Peckham, New Cross, Deptford, Greenwich & Lewisham

Key

❶ Waterloo Station

❷ King's College Hospital

❸ Stuart Arms/Newlands Tavern

❹ Goldsmiths College

❺ Albany Empire

❻ White Swan

❼ Lewisham Gaumont

DENMARK HILL

Expecting to give birth in December 1969, Yoko Ono miscarried at **King's College Hospital** on Bessemer Road, Denmark Hill, on 12 October, three days after being admitted. There was much happier news for John Lennon's fellow Beatle Paul McCartney and his wife Linda, on 13 September 1971, when their daughter Stella was born at the same hospital. Inspired by the birth, McCartney named his band Wings. Stella is now one of the world's top fashion designers.

PECKHAM

Now called the **Stuart Arms**, on Stuart Road, this Peckham pub used to be called the **Newlands Tavern** and was a popular pub rock venue. Graham Parker and the Rumour rehearsed and made their debut here. And the tavern was a regular gig for Ian Dury's Kilburn and the High Roads, Dr Feelgood and Flip City, a hard-working pub rock combo on London's pub circuit featuring Declan MacManus, the future Elvis Costello, on guitar and vocals.

At the end of the summer of 1964, Syd Barrett of Pink Floyd prepared to move down to London from his native Cambridge to study painting at Camberwell Art School in Peckham. That same summer he tried LSD for the first time. Pulp frontman Jarvis Cocker lived at 59 Lyndhurst Grove while studying at St Martin's.

NEW CROSS

A number of rock'n'roll luminaries have attended **Goldsmiths College** on Lewisham Way. Velvet Underground's only British-born member, John Cale, attended Goldsmiths and later the Royal Academy of Music, before winning a scholarship at Tanglewood, one of America's foremost music colleges. Other ex-Goldsmiths students include Brian Molko of Placebo, Steve Mackey of Pulp and dub poet Linton Kwesi Johnson, a former sociology student who graduated in 1973. Dire Straits' bassist John Illsley also studied sociology around 1977–78 and has been an honorary fellow of the college since 1996. The Bonzo Dog Doo-Dah Band also formed here.

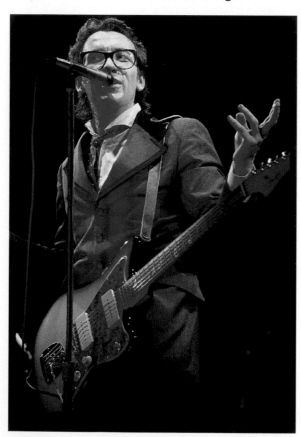

Below: Elvis Costello appeared at the Albany Empire under the alias Otis Westinghouse.

Sex Pistols' manager Malcolm McLaren left the college in 1971 without completing his degree. Allegedly, he set the library on fire whilst attending Goldsmiths although nothing was proved. Brit-poppers Blur were formed when Alex James and Graham Coxon met at the college around 1987. James studied French and Coxon Fine Art. One of their first gigs as Blur (after ditching the name Seymour) was the 1989 degree show in which Damien Hirst and other young British

Above: Mark Perry, a bank clerk from Deptford, razored his suits and embraced punk by starting the first punk rock fanzine, *Sniffin' Glue*.

artists exhibited. In 1999 Blur went back to Goldsmiths to perform in the Students Union, which was filmed by LWT for *The South Bank Show*. John Wardle (better known as Public Image Limited's Jah Wobble) currently lectures at Goldsmiths. And with many Goldsmiths students involved in bands and other music projects the list is set to increase.

DEPTFORD

Dire Straits formed in the Spring of 1977, when bassist John Illsley shared a flat in Deptford with Mark and David Knopfler. Also from the area were Squeeze, most of whom – Jools Holland, Chris Difford and Glenn Tilbrook – grew up in Deptford and appeared on the Deptford Fun City record label. Holland once penned a solo single called 'Broadway Boogie', which was all about the dubious pleasures of Deptford Broadway. Squeeze cast their net wider in other songs: 'Cool for Cats' was a real London record that mentioned a number of capital locations including Wandsworth and Heathrow Airport.

When Jools Holland left the band, they played five nights at the now defunct **Albany Empire**. The support act was billed as Otis Westinghouse and the Mystery Elevators. On the first night, there were only about four people in the audience. Otis turned out to be no less than Elvis Costello and the Attractions. Needless to say, word got around, and it was soon packed. The two bands shared the stage for the last hour of the show.

GREENWICH

A pub called the **White Swan**, at 65–67 Greenwich High Road, proved to be the inspiration for Dire Straits' first single and breakthrough song, 'Sultans of Swing'. In the summer of 1977 Mark Knopfler wrote his first hit after seeing a jazz group playing at this pub, going through jazz tunes in their weekly residency.

LEWISHAM

Lewisham Gaumont (re-named Odeon in 1962) at Loampit Vale on Lewisham High Street was a cinema-cum-live music venue throughout the 1960s and 1970s. The Beatles played twice here in 1963. Rod Stewart's solo album *Smiler* received a boost when Paul and Linda McCartney made an unexpected appearance at the Faces show at the Odeon in November 1974. 'I've got my brother and sister coming on stage with me now,' Stewart told a bemused audience. 'My brother with a humped back and my sister with one leg. They're gonna come on and sing a song.' The crowd erupted as the McCartneys launched into a number with Rod. It was levelled in 1982 to make way for a delightful town centre.

Below: AC/DC's Bon Scott died in the back of a car in Dulwich but the group carried on, including their guitarist Angus Young, shown here.

DULWICH

Bon Scott, lead singer of the Australian heavy rock band AC/DC, was found dead in February 1980, in a car outside a friend's house in Overhill Road. Scott died after drinking until 3 a.m. at the Music Machine, now the Camden Palace (see Camden). A friend drove him home, but when they arrived he found Scott couldn't be moved. The friend drove back to his own place with the singer in the car.

Above: The site of what was the Three Tuns pub. A back room housed the Beckenham Arts Lab, which was frequented by David Bowie.

Still Scott couldn't be woken, so he was covered with a blanket and was left to sleep it off in the car. Some 15 hours later the friend went down to check on Scott but he still wasn't moving. He had choked on his own vomit and the coroner recorded he'd drunk himself to death.

BECKENHAM

In 1969, David Bowie helped set up the Beckenham Arts Lab in the back room above the Three Tuns pub on the High Street, now the Rat and Parrot. Then, he lived in Beckenham, at 24 Foxgrove Road. The Arts Lab was designed as a performance space and meeting house, a place for theatre groups to spout Jean Genet and listen to rhythm and blues music. The idea was to encourage local people to congregate and get involved in all aspects of the arts. Later that year, Bowie shared a large communal Victorian mansion called Haddon Hall at 42 Southend Road, now demolished, with his fiancée Angie Barnett. He wrote a number of songs while living there, including a lot of material for *Ziggy Stardust* and *Hunky Dory*, the cover of which was shot in the garden.

BROMLEY

Bromley's ability to spawn rock'n'roll superstars is not immediately apparent (Fatboy Slim, a.k.a. Norman Cook, and Clash drummer Topper Headon). But so many writers, artists and musicians seem to hail from suburbia, for no other reason than there's so much to rebel against: the blandness, the boredom, the uniform conformity. Little wonder then that Bromley was one of the cradles of punk rock. Around 1975, early punk Siouxsie Sioux started to meet people she could relate to, folk such as Steve Severin, Billy Idol and Simon Barker. She and her friends became known as the 'Bromley Contingent' and were hugely influential in punk. They went to every Sex Pistols' gig and Siouxsie Sioux often stood out thanks to her fishnet stockings and swastika armband. They were first inspired by a Pistols' gig at Bromley Tech in January 1976. She later fronted Siouxsie and the Banshees, joined by Steve Severin. Siouxsie Sioux was brought up as Susan Dallion in nearby Chislehurst and her song 'Hong Kong Garden' was penned in homage to a local Chinese take-away of the same name.

Bromley's most famous former resident is David Bowie. He spent his early days in what he has described as 'emotionally sub-zero households' at 23 Clarence Road and 106 Canon Road. In 1957 his parents moved to 4 Plaistow Grove in Sundridge Park, where Bowie lived for ten years during his years at Bromley Technical High School (now Ravensbourne School for boys) in Oakley Road. He left in 1963. One of Bowie's teachers at Bromley Technical High School was the father of Beckenham's other great rock'n'roll hero, guitarist and singer Peter Frampton, who himself attended this school.

Frampton was born in Beckenham in 1950 and went on to form Humble Pie with Steve Marriott of the Small Faces in 1969. His 1976 live album *Frampton Comes Alive* is still the best-selling live album of all time. Later, Frampton survived a serious car crash and in 1987 was Bowie's lead guitarist on his Glass Spider tour.

CROYDON

Newspaper columnists detest it and Beckenham's finest, David Bowie, once described it as his nemesis: 'I hated Croydon with a real vengeance,' Bowie said in an interview many years later. 'It represented everything I didn't want in my life, everything I wanted to get away from. It was gonna be the big second city to London, but it never came to be. They put up these awful faceless office blocks, complete concrete hell.'

Croydon has never just been full of concrete. The foundations of the punk band the Damned were laid when drummer Christopher Miller met old Croydon friend guitarist Ray Burns at Croydon's Fairfield Halls in Park Lane. Miller renamed himself Rat Scabies after a bout of the disease and Burns became Captain Sensible. The

Right: The Damned were formed when Rat Scabies met Captain Sensible at the Fairfield Halls (below).

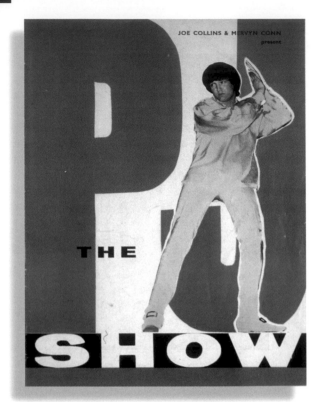

JOE COLLINS & MERVYN CONN present

THE PJ SHOW

Above: PJ Proby was banned from Croydon's ABC chain in the mid-1960s.

band members chose wacky names so they could keep signing on for unemployment benefit. Scabies was a nice middle-class boy whose father was secretary of the Wagner Society and whose younger brother shot pistols competitively for England. He worked as a porter at the Fairfield Halls, where he used to clean the toilets. The Halls remain a popular south London concert venue and have featured such top soul stars as Martha Reeves, Mary Wilson and Edwin Starr. The venue was the scene of important early UK shows by bluesmen such as Howlin' Wolf, Sonny Boy Williamson and Muddy Waters. In October 1963, at the American Blues Festival, Eric Clapton got a chance to play with Muddy Waters, Memphis Slim and Willie Dixon. Two years later, Buddy Guy, Roosevelt Sykes and Mississippi Fred McDowell were among the acts appearing. Pink Floyd played here in 1970 and the Beatles performed twice here in 1963, the first time in April as part of Brian Epstein's Mersey Beat Showcase and again in September.

Croydon's ABC Theatre chain once banned the American singer PJ Proby from concerts when the trouser seam of his velvet trousers split at the crotch while on stage in January 1965. He was pilloried by the newspapers for his sins.

DARTFORD

If Dartford hadn't existed would someone have invented it? If Dartford hadn't existed would there have been the Rolling Stones? Both Mick Jagger and Keith Richards are natives of Dartford; both were born at Livingstone Hospital on East Hill and both grew up within a stone's throw of each other. Keith Richards spent his early years at **33 Chastillian Road**, before the family uprooted to the new council estate at Temple Hill. Mick Jagger's childhood home was close by at **39 Denver Road**. Jagger and Richards first met as youngsters in the early 1950s at **Wentworth Primary School** on James Road.

In 1954, Keith Richards and his family moved from **6 Spielman Road**, Temple Hill. A little later, the Jagger family moved to a larger house in Wilmington, at which point the future Glimmer Twins lost touch. Richards attended **Dartford Technical School** on Miskin Road in the late 1950s, while Jagger went to Dartford Grammar at West Hill. In 1961, while in their late teens, they were united again by coincidence on the London-bound platform at Dartford train station. Jagger was going to a lecture at the London School of Economics and Richards to Sidcup Art College. But sod the studies, more importantly they realized they shared a common passion for blues music. Mick was holding a Chuck Berry single when they met again.

While at school in the 1950s, Jagger had a holiday job at **Bexley Hospital** on Old Bexley Lane, where he lost his virginity to a nurse in a hospital cupboard. Coincidentally, girlfriend Marianne Faithfull later spent months in the same hospital in 1969, to cure her heroin addiction. Boy George was born here in June 1961, but later grew up in Eltham – 29 Joan Crescent to be precise.

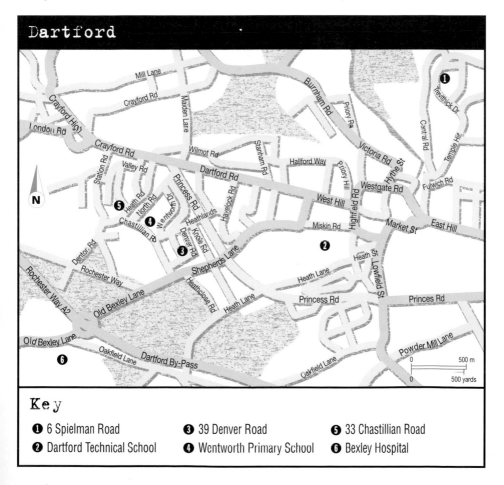

Key

❶ 6 Spielman Road
❷ Dartford Technical School
❸ 39 Denver Road
❹ Wentworth Primary School
❺ 33 Chastillian Road
❻ Bexley Hospital

Bibliography/ Further reading

The following is a list of source material used during the research of this book and a guide to further, and in some cases, essential reading.

Barnes, Richard, *The Making of Tommy*. Trinifold.

Bacon, Tony, *London Live*. Balafon, 1999.

Bangs, Lester, *Psychotic Reactions And Carburetor Dung*. Minerva, 1990.

Bird, Brian, *Skiffle: The Story of Folk Song with a Jazz Beat*. Robert Hale, 1958.

Booth, Stanley, *The True Adventures of The Rolling Stones*. Heinemann, 1985.

Buckley, David, *No Mercy: The Authorised and Uncensored Biography of The Stranglers*. Hodder & Stoughton, 1998.

Buckley, Jonathan, et al, *Rock: The Rough Guide*. Rough Guides, 1999.

Burchill, Julie and Parsons, Tony, *The Boy Looked at Johnny: The Obituary of Rock and Roll*. Pluto, 1978.

Clayton-Lea, Tony, *Elvis Costello: A Biography*. Andre Deutsch, 1998.

Coleman, Ray, *Rod Stewart: The Biography*. Pavilion, 1994.

Coleman, Ray with Wyman, Bill, *Stone Alone*. Viking, 1990.

Collin, Matthew, *Altered State: The Story of Ecstasy Culture and Acid House*. Serpent's Tail, 1997.

Coon, Caroline, *1988: The New Wave Punk Rock Explosion*. Omnibus Press, 1982.

Crimp, Susan and Burstein, Patricia, *The Many Lives of Elton John*. Robert Hale, 1992.

Davies, Ray, *X-Ray: The Unauthorised Autobiography*. Viking, 1994.

Davies, Dave, Kink. *Boxtree*, 1996.

Davis, Stephen, *Hammer of The Gods: Led Zeppelin Unauthorised*. Sidgwick & Jackson, 1985.

Dolgins, Adam, *Rock Names: How Rock Groups Got Their Names*. Pan Macmillan, 1994.

Etchingham, Kathy, *Through Gypsy Eyes: My Life, The Sixties and Jimi Hendrix*. Gollancz, 1998.

Farson, Daniel, *Soho In The Fifties*. Michael Joseph, 1987.

Frame, Pete, *Rockin' Around Britain*. Omnibus, 1999.

Frame, Pete, *Complete Rock Family Trees*. Omnibus, 1980.

Fletcher, Tony, *Dear Boy: The Life of Keith Moon*. Omnibus, 1998.

Geller, Deborah, *The Brian Epstein Story*. Faber & Faber, 2000.

Godbolt, Jim, *Jazz in Britain 1919–1959*. Quartet, 1984.

Green, Jonathon, *Days In The Life: Voices From The London Underground 1961–1971*. Pimlico, 1998.

Heath, Chris, *Pet Shop Boys, Literally*. Viking, 1990.

Humphreys, Rob, *Rough Guide to London*. Rough Guides, 1999.

Heckstall-Smith, Dick, *The Safest Place in the World: A Personal History of British Rhythm and Blues*. Quartet, 1989.

Hewitt, Paolo, *Small Faces: The Young Mods. Forgotten Story*. Acid Jazz.

Jackson, Laura, *Queen and I – The Brian May Story*. Smith Gryphon, 1994.

Jones, Lesley-Ann, *Freddie Mercury, The Definitive Biography*. Hodder & Stoughton, 1997.

Kent, Nick, *The Dark Stuff: Selected Writings on Rock Music, 1972-1993*. Penguin, 1994.

Larkin, Colin, *All Time Top 1000 Albums*. Guinness Publishing, 1994.

Low, Crail and Minto, Lucy, *The Handbook Guide to Rock & Pop London*. Handbook Publishing, 1997.

Lydon, John, *Rotten: No Irish, No Blacks, No Dogs*. Hodder & Stoughton, 1993.

MacDonald, Ian, *Revolution In T he Head: The Beatles. Records And The Sixties*. Fourth Estate, 1994.

Mankowitz, Gered, *Mason's Yard to Primrose Hill*. Genesis Publications, 1995.

McGill, Angus, *London Pub Guide*. Pavilion, 1995.

McDevitt, Chas, *Skiffle: The Definitive Inside Story*. Robson, 1997.

McLagan, Ian, *All The Rage*. Pan, 2000.

Napier-Bell, Simon, *You Don't Have to Say You Love Me*. Ebury Press, 1998.

Norman, Philip, *Shout! The True Story of The Beatles*. Hamish Hamilton, 1981.

Oldham, Andrew Loog, *Stoned*. Secker & Warburg, 2000.

Palacios, Julian, *Lost in the Woods: Syd Barrett and The Pink Floyd*. Boxtree, 1998.

Palmer, Myles, *Mark Knopfler: An Unauthorised Biography*. Sidgwick & Jackson, 1991.

Palmer, Tony, *All You Need Is Love: The Story of Popular Music*. Weidenfeld & Nicolson, 1976.

Paytress, Mark, *Twentieth Century Boy: The Marc Bolan Story*. Sidgwick & Jackson.

Platt, John, *London's Rock Routes*. Fourth Estate, 1985.

Price, Simon, *Everything: A Book About Manic Street Preachers*. Virgin, 1999.

Rawlings, Terry, *Rock on Wood (The Origin of a Rock & Roll Face)*. Boxtree, 1999.

Reed, Jeremy, *Waiting for the Man (A Biography of Lou Reed)*. Picador, 1994.

Rimmer, Dave, *Like Punk Never Happened*. Faber & Faber, 1985.

Rogan, Johnny, *Morrissey & Marr: The Severed Alliance*. Omnibus, 1993.

Savage, Jon, *England's Dreaming: Sex Pistols and Punk Rock*. Faber & Faber, 1991.

Schaffner, Nicholas, *Saucerful of Secrets: The Pink Floyd Odyssey*. Sidgwick & Jackson, 1991.

Schreuders, Piet, Lewisohn, Mark & Smith, Adam, *The Beatles London*. Hamlyn, 1994.

Shapiro, Harry, *Eric Clapton: Lost in the Blues*. Guinness Publishing, 1992.

Spicer, Al, *Rock: 100 Essential CDs*. Rough Guides, 1999.

Tobler, John and Frame, Pete, *25 Years of Rock*. Optimum, 1980.

Index

Acknowledgements

The author would like to thank the London Borough of Wandsworth, the Merton Library Services and the Newspaper Library in Colindale. Also thanks to Roy Addison, Frank Barrett, Tim Clifford, Suzanne Elston, Jamie Fox, Simon Hartley, Terry Howard, Martha Larkin, Malcolm McLaren, Annie Mills, Keith Morris, John Otway, David Painter, Mike Persson, David Prest, Carol Richardson, Heidi Seetzen, Melissa Shales, Michael Sherwin, Mick Thompson and Roger Tagholm.

Dedication

This book is dedicated to Geezer Mohammed.

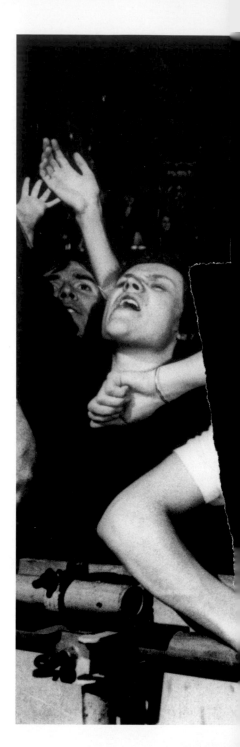

Picture credits

Grateful thanks to all the record companies that gave permission for the reproduction of the various record sleeves. Also, thanks to Soho Records, Berwick Street, London, who kindly provided memorabilia. Every effort has been made by the Publishers to trace the copyright holders of record cover artworks reproduced in this book.

The author and the publishers extend their thanks to the following who loaned their photographs for inclusion in this book:

Ray Burmiston: p8; p23; p39 (t); p46 (b); p84; p85; p97; p106; p112; p132; p133; p150; p156; p157; p163; p174.

Richard Holt: p90. Reproduced by kind permission of Abbey Road Studios.

The Hulton Archive Picture Collection: p13; 17; 18-19; p31; p57; p59 (b); p63; p71; p75; p77; p99; p123; p137; p148; p149; p167.

Keith Morris: p24; p45; p49; p73; p117; p119; p131; p139; p161; p172; p191.

Redferns Music Picture Collection: p38; p51; p52; p69; p101; 128; p145; p169.

Gulen Shevki: P124; p125.

World Attractions Ltd: p6; (David Parkinson) p5.